Lyn   psychotherapist who specializes in personal and group development. She is author of nine titles, including the bestselling *60 Ways to Feel Amazing* and *60 Ways to Change Your Life*. In addition to giving seminars and workshops, she writes a weekly column for a major Internet provider, as well as articles for a variety of national magazines. She lives in Essex, UK.

Visit Lynda online at www.lyndafield.com

By the same author:

60 Ways to Change Your Life

60 Ways to Feel Amazing

The Little Book of Woman Power

60 Tips for Self-Esteem

Creating Self-Esteem

60 Ways to Heal Your Life

More than 60 Ways to Make Your Life Amazing

Self-Esteem for Women

The Self-Esteem Workbook

Just Do It Now!

How to become the person
you most want to be

Lynda Field

Vermilion
LONDON

10

First published in 2001 by Vermilion,
an imprint of Ebury Press, Random House,
20 Vauxhall Bridge Road, London SW1V 2SA

Addresses for companies within the Random House Group
Limited can be found at: www.randomhouse.co.uk/offices.htm

The Random House Group Limited Reg. No. 954009

Papers used by Vermilion are natural, recyclable
products made from wood grown in sustainable forests.

Printed and bound in Great Britain by
CPI Antony Rowe, Chippenham, Wiltshire

A CIP catalogue record for this book is available from
the British Library

The Random House Group Limited supports The Forest Stewardship
Council (FSC), the leading international forest certification organisation.
All our titles that are printed on Greenpeace approved FSC certified paper
carry the FSC logo. Our paper procurement policy can be found at:
www.randomhouse.co.uk/environment

ISBN 9780091876296

This book is dedicated to my wonderful father,
Idwal Iestyn Goronwy, who taught me how to
make the most of my life.

Acknowledgements

My thanks and love to all of my family, who are such an inspiring crowd:

Richard, who is the best husband, father and stepfather in the world;

Jack and Alex, sons I can be proud of;

Leilah my lovely daughter and her baby, my beautiful granddaughter Alaska;

My stepson Bevan Ward;

My parents Barbara and Idwal Goronwy and my mother-in law Mary Field, all powerfully creative role models;

My brother, Trevor Goronwy, his wife Sholpan and their enchanting son Daniel;

My sister-in-law Maggie Rance and her children, Polly, Michael, William and Nicholas.

To old friends and new, especially Barbara Higham, Gill Widdows and Sue Roberts.

To all at Ebury Press of Random House, who are a delight to work with, and with special thanks to Judith Kendra, who does what she does so very well.

And to all my readers and clients who provide a continual source of inspiration.

Contents

Acknowledgements   VI
Tasks   VIII
Preface   IX

Introduction   1

SECTION 1:
CREATING YOUR OWN REALITY
1   Energy Matters   6
2   The Magic in Your Life   14
3   The Power of Belief   28
4   Slug Slime, Trees That Can Smell and Collective
     Consciousness   46
5   Creative Visualization   57

SECTION 2:
TRANSFORMING YOUR LIFE
6   What Sort of Realities Are You Creating?   72
7   Overcoming Your Obstacles   84
8   Finding Harmony and Balance   96
9   Loving Your Life   115

SECTION 3:
LIVING DYNAMICALLY
10   Begin It Now!   132
11   A New Self-Image   142
12   Creating Amazing Relationships   158
13   Improving Your Health and Fitness Levels   176
14   Increasing Your Wealth   193
15   Discovering Your Life's Work   208

Conclusion   225

References and Further Reading   226
Index   228

Tasks

1 In Search of Positivity   7
2 Feeling Your Own Energy   10
3 Feeling the Energy of Others   11
4 Recognizing the Meaningful Nature of
   Coincidences   17
5 Getting What You Want   20
6 Absorbing the Life Force   22
7 Feeling the Good Vibrations   24
8 Your Unconscious at Work   31
9 Your Self-Image   34
10 Your World View   41
11 Holding the Biggest Thought   42
12 Becoming Conscious   50
13 Becoming More Telepathic   53
14 Getting Into a State of Relaxation   63
15 Creating a New Reality   68
16 Assessing Your Life Zones   77
17 Rising to the Challenge   86
18 Your Positive Affirmations   90
19 Stopping Doing   102
20 Discovering Your Core Belief   103
21 Changing Your Mind   104
22 Coming out of Denial   108
23 6 Ways Towards Becoming Assertive   111
24 Listening to Your Intuition   118
25 Drawing Your Lifeline   119
26 Opening Your Heart   121
27 4 Steps to Forgiveness   123
28 The Best That Can Happen   135
29 Transforming Energy   138
30 Your Love List   139

Preface

If there were dreams to sell what would you buy? What would you love to have in your life? A fabulous home, luxurious holidays, a successful career, loving relationships, a happy family, good health ... Yes, these things and many more are on offer, and you can have them all. But be warned, none of them can guarantee you the *ultimate experience* which you are seeking and without which you will never feel fulfilled. So what is it that will ensure a life of happiness, joy, contentment, inspiration, satisfaction and fulfilment? What is it that can bring this magic to your days?

When we are feeling motivated and fascinated our lives flow easily and no challenge is too great to overcome. Think back to a time when you were excited and inspired by something: a project, an idea, a person ... Now, remember how this felt. It was an amazing feeling wasn't it? You were full of enthusiasm, direction and purpose. On such a day you really can appreciate how good it feels to be alive. It may have been a long time since you experienced this sense of *aliveness* in your life. And this, of course, is the ultimate experience, which money can't buy and dreams don't necessarily bring.

Why do you think you are here, on planet Earth; what is your purpose?

This isn't a trick question, I want you to try to answer it.

Well, it *might* be so that you can grow up, buy a house, have a family, go to work, mow the lawn, pay the bills, put out the cat, go to bed, get up and start all over again. And certainly this is life, these are the things we do. But there is something more and you know what it is! The true purpose of your visit to Earth is *to realize your full potential as a human being.* This means that whilst you are putting out or bringing in the cat you are experiencing the drive and enthusiasm of a person who lives their life to the full and makes the most of every opportunity to develop and grow.

> *When you make the most of your self*
> *you make the most of your life.*

And that is what this book is all about. Dreams can come true and your life can become more interesting and fascinating than you could ever possibly imagine. *Just Do It Now!* will show you how to become the person you most want to be.

Lynda Field

Introduction

'*I don't want to get to the end of my life and find I just lived the length of it. I want to have lived the width of it as well.*'

DIANE ACKERMAN

Yes, you continually turn up to keep your appointments with life: work; relationships; dentist; family ... You keep putting in the hours and living the length, but what about the width? How satisfied are you? Is life pretty good to you at the moment or are you facing flat, one-dimensional and monochromatic boredom when you long for glorious Technicolor experiences with fascinating depths and dimensions? Check out your present satisfaction levels in the different areas of your life. The Life Zone Checklist on page 2 will help you to see where you stand.

The scale of feelings from 1 to 8 represents the range of emotions from your lowest to your highest satisfaction levels. Don't spend too much time deliberating over your answers, just quickly tick off the number which most relates to your feelings in your different zones.

How did you do? If *any* of your answers are below 6 then this book is for you. Anything below 6 demonstrates that you are operating below your potential. In the words of my old school reports you '*could do better*'. Don't see this as a judgement but as a wonderful and liberating truth. You wouldn't dream of struggling to live by candlelight when you have electric power. And so why would you accept limited satisfaction levels in your love life, career prospects, financial reward, self-image ... etc. when you have the power to charge your life with excitement, energy, enthusiasm and aliveness? Come on, what have you got to lose?

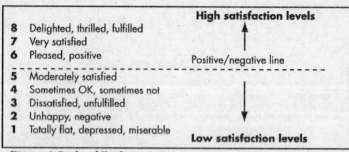

		High satisfaction levels
8	Delighted, thrilled, fulfilled	
7	Very satisfied	
6	Pleased, positive	Positive/negative line
5	Moderately satisfied	
4	Sometimes OK, sometimes not	
3	Dissatisfied, unfulfilled	
2	Unhappy, negative	
1	Totally flat, depressed, miserable	**Low satisfaction levels**

Figure 1 Scale of Feelings

Life zone	1	2	3	4	5	6	7	8
Self-image								
Love								
Family								
Friends								
Health and fitness								
Money								
Work								

Figure 2 Life Zone Checklist

Decide to make the most of your life: decide to *Just Do It Now!*

Look back at Figure 1 and notice the positive/negative line between numbers 5 and 6. This denotes a critical change in attitude from being *moderately satisfied* (position 5) *to being pleased, positive* (position 6). We are either positive or not, there is no place in between. We can't feel slightly negative or a bit positive, we are one or the other. Any answer below 6 in your Life Zone Checklist is based in negativity and 6 and above take you into a positive cycle of growth, enthusiasm and fulfilment.

The whole world seems to be telling us to 'just be positive' and 'not to be so negative' as if our personal problems can be waved away by a magic wand. These messages are starting to sound like glossy media hype and the real meaning behind the terms positive and negative have been lost. So this book is not going to tell you to 'just get positive and everything will be all right'. I want to take you behind the scenes of annoying, clichéd, upbeat chat to show you how:

YOU HAVE HELPED TO CREATE YOUR PRESENT CIRCUMSTANCES

YOU CAN TRANSFORM YOUR LIFE

YOU CAN FEEL GLAD TO BE ALIVE – EVERY DAY

YOU CAN ATTRACT SUCCESS

YOU CAN BE THE PERSON YOU MOST WANT TO BE

Section 1: Creating Your Own Reality

This is a step-by-step guide to the simple principles which lie behind the incredible truth that *we are not slaves to our destiny*. Yes, we really do create our life scenarios and attract circumstances, events and even people into our lives, by just being the way we are. We will discover exactly *how* and *why* we create difficulties and challenges in our love lives, family relationships, friendships, work prospects and finances; in fact, in every area of our lives. Of course, this is a *'how to'* book and so the emphasis will always be on how to apply the principles that we learn to change our lives for the better.

Section 2: Transforming Your Life

This section will focus on the exact ways that we can overcome any obstacles and limitations that we encounter. Whenever our vision of *who we are* fails to match our vision of *who we want to be* there is only one way to bridge the gap – we must change. We will look at the mechanics of change and why we sometimes carry on behaving in the same old way (even though it doesn't work) just because we are so afraid of change. Section 2 also examines the power and magic of mind energy: did you know that a positive condition is always a magnetic condition and that this magnetism brings the power of magic into our lives?

Section 3: Living Dynamically

Living dynamically really means that we are *just doing it!* That is, we have decided to make the very most of our lives, every day and in every way. We know that this is not a dress rehearsal; this is it, our precious life, and we are no longer prepared to accept second best. Here we look back at the Life Zone Checklist and learn exactly how to lift all our scores above the positive/negative line so that they are all 6 or above. In this final section you can create your own blueprint for success in every area of your life.

Just Do It Now! is a practical book based on holistic principles. This means that we will be looking at *all* aspects of the self that we bring to each and every one of our experiences. You are so much more than you think you are: you are a powerhouse of amazing energy. You are Mind, Body, Spirit and Emotion and each of these interrelated aspects of your self contributes to the powerful, creative energy that is yours alone.

In my Internet role as inspirational writer, personal development counsellor and online life coach I receive a lot of feedback. Where I have used case studies, FAQs (frequently asked questions) and other examples, I have changed all names to maintain confidentiality. There are numerous practical tips and techniques scattered throughout the book and all of these have been tried, tested and well used by myself, my readers and my clients.

The various *tasks* in the book introduce original and easy-to-use ways to increase your levels of energy and awareness. They have been designed to focus on your own unique and specific needs, and I hope you will find them good fun to do, as well as fascinating to experience.

It is said that we teach what we need to learn, and writing this book has been a wonderful experience for me. It often surprises people to discover that self-help gurus have their own problems! We all learn by overcoming personal challenges and that is as true for me as it is for you. *Just Do It Now!* was an amazing title to work with. How could I ever procrastinate when a little voice in my head kept whispering, 'Oh, for goodness' sake, Lynda, just write it!'? I hope that you feel motivated and supported as you read this book. May you become inspired to reach your highest potential and to live the wonderful life that you deserve.

Creating Your Own Reality

Energy matters

'Hope springs eternal in the human breast ...'

ALEXANDER POPE

As a writer of inspirational and motivational books, people are naturally curious to know if I walk my talk; if I am a 'positive' person. Most often I am, but not always. Even though I know all about positive psychology theory and I have written enough tips and techniques to last several lifetimes, it is sometimes hard not to drift down that old well-worn path of self-doubt and negative energy: we all seem to carry within us a very damaging inclination to criticize ourselves.

Think of a day that was going well: the sun was out, you felt good and full of beans, everything was fine ... and then something happened which blew your sense of well-being clean away. It was probably a very minor incident but it undermined your positive feelings by questioning your right to feel so good about yourself and the world. You know how it goes only too well. A slither of doubt: *does she like me; have I said too much/too little; am I up to finishing this project; should I say what I really think; is this skirt too short for me; have I bitten off more than I can chew; is he criticizing me; is this the right decision ...?* And down you go, spiralling into a whirlpool of negativity. Whatever happened to your upbeat mood? How could such strong and powerful energy evaporate so quickly? It's easy to understand why some people have become cynical about the benefits of positivity. Isn't it true that, when we are feeling down, the most irritating and useless advice we can hear is all that stuff about looking on the bright side of life? We are hurting and we want sympathy and truckloads of it. *No it's not fair; you didn't deserve that; what a shame; it's all so and so's fault; it's quite wrong that you should be treated so badly; poor old you, let's have a cup of tea.* Ah, that's better, now we are beginning to feel understood and appreciated again. But then, after the tea and sympathy and our support group has gone home, we start to look around for a shot of hope. Hope opens doors which have been closed, brings a lightness to our step, gives us back our meaning and purpose and, thankfully, springs eternal in most of our breasts. I always think of hope as the natural antidote to self-criticism: a wonderful elixir that lifts us over that positive/negative line to ensure that yet again we can bounce back with a smile.

The point is that when we are needing a dose of positivity it seems pretty elusive. We can't put our finger on it, one minute it's here and then its gone: we can't contain it and measure it out. But we can see it and feel it and experience the results of it. You might wonder what it looks like. Try Task 1 when you are next out and about amongst people.

TASK 1 ....

In Search of Positivity

Go out and look for it. Observe others closely, listen carefully to the words they speak and the tone they use. Watch the way that people carry themselves, become aware of body language and facial expressions. These are just a few indicators to start you off on your investigations.

....

What did you discover? Did you find much positive energy? If you look hard enough it's possible to find out so much about another person: a fearful look in the eye, a bright glint, an uplifted spirit, a downcast face and body, an open, helpful expression, a closed, shuttered look, an upright confident walk, a victim's shuffle, meaningful eye contact, evasive expression, upbeat tone of voice, angry tone, victim's whine ...

yes, the whole of the energy of the universe (the positive and the negative) is there to see if we bother to look.

So in a way we *can* measure positivity because we can see it in action. We can also feel this energy; people carry it with them. Who do you call when you're feeling fed up? Who do you know who can always brighten your mood? These people can lift our spirits by the power of the energy field that surrounds them: they can enter a room and everyone lightens up. You don't have to be clairvoyant to see these energy fields – you saw them when you were out observing.

Things Are Not What They Seem

Absolutely everything in the universe is made of energy: it creates all the structures and elements that go to form our reality. Nobel Laureate Max Planck discovered that everything that exists vibrates and, at a sub-atomic level, all matter is energy. When you look around your room and see the door, the dog, this book, your body ... you are seeing objects which seem entirely separate and different from each other. But in fact the basic building blocks of your dog, this book and everything else you are looking at are identical. You are made of the same thing as a tree, the clouds, a flower, the TV, a beetle, your friend, your enemy ... now, this really does take some thinking about, doesn't it? Furthermore, this 'solid' world which we see before us is not at all solid. Everything in existence is made entirely of atoms, each of which consists of a tiny nucleus, with a few very tiny particles, called electrons, orbiting around it.

Celia Wright, discussing energy medicine in the *Higher Nature News*, tells us the following amazing fact:

'Astonishingly, if you took all the matter in our bodies and stuck it together with no spaces in between, it would all pack into one little toe, and the rest of us would be empty.'

Astonishing indeed! Atoms are in fact energy fields possessing positive, negative and neutral charges and they produce electric and magnetic forces. Our universe is made of this pure energy which has created all the structures, forms and elements which go to create our reality. Think of the universe as a huge ocean of vibrating energy which creates all forms of existence. This essential energy (the essence of all things) is vibrating at different speeds and so creates the different forms of matter, from fine to dense.

Modern physics has confirmed what ancient spiritual and mystical traditions have always taught: *our physical universe is not made of matter but is made of energy. All forms of energy are interrelated and have an effect on each other.* The implications of these scientific truths are far reaching and utterly staggering. Everything is connected (literally) and this means that the way we think, feel and act must have a profound effect on other people. Similarly, we are closely influenced by the thoughts, feelings and actions of everyone around us. We shall go on to see how our thoughts and feelings actually create form (matter) and how the people and events in our lives really do walk through the doors of our expectations.

Becoming Aware

Let's just go back to that little toe for a moment. When I first read this account of all my 'matter' fitting into such a tiny space I found myself continually looking at my little toe in wonder. Many times during the following days in the midst of the hurly burly of my life – dishes, driving, swimming, cooking, writing, reading, talking, washing, doing nothing – I would suddenly remember and each time it stopped me in my tracks. I also wanted to share this revelation with everyone I met. So I wasn't this solid body who needed energy to get up and go: I was energy. All matter is energy. Once you know this the world can look like a different place. Certain people such as clairvoyants, yogis and some healers can see this energy but there are many other ways to observe it. Remember Task 1, which asked you to become aware of positive energy; you were able to recognize positivity (and negativity) very easily. Once you start to become aware of your own energy and the energy of other living things you will enter a new, exciting, dynamic and empowering phase of your life.

TASK 2 ....

Feeling Your Own Energy

Sit quietly and contemplate the idea that you are not solid matter but a vibrating body of energy. Now rub your hands briskly together for about a minute and then hold your palms so that they are almost touching. Can you feel the tingling of the energy fields between your hands? Now be aware of this energy as you slowly move your hands away from each other and then move them back towards each other. Experiment with these movements and see what you can feel. It might help you to concentrate if you close your eyes. Feel this energy whenever you have a spare moment and remind yourself that you *are* energy.

....

Suffering in Style

The next time you are feeling fed up I want you to *really* feel fed up. This means that you don't just sit and moan and feel miserable but that you sit and close your eyes and feel your energy. This heavy, depressed feeling is your *energetic* response to whatever is going on. If you are enjoying your misery (and who doesn't enjoy a good wallow every now and again?) then just get into your energy and stay with it for as long as you like. Sometimes when I feel like this I tell my family that I'm disappearing for a while and that I'm going under the duvet. And I do just that. I get into bed, pull the duvet over my head and have a good old miserable time. And somehow this changes things as my energy shifts into an upward gear and I start to come out of my mood.

However, if you aren't in for a good energy slump (you are nowhere near your bed or you just want to feel better quickly), simply link with the power of your energy. Recognize that you can change your mood by lifting your awareness. Look to your small toe and remember that you are part of the amazing flow of universal energy; see the bigger picture and leave your depressing mood behind. Say the following affirmation:

Universal energy flows through me.

As you practise becoming aware of energy you will start to feel more lively and responsive. Watch for changes in your life as your awareness develops and grows.

TASK 3 ....

Feeling the Energy of Others

If you hold your palm close to the palm of another person you can feel their energy too. Find someone who will try this out with you. Move your hands around the outline of your friend's body. Without touching her, trace the energy right around her outer edges. What can you feel? Move your hands further away and experience any changes. Closing your eyes might help you to become more sensitive. There is no right and wrong way to do this, just become aware of her energy. Change over and then compare your findings. Isn't it incredible to discover that you are so much more than you thought you were? Here you are actually feeling someone else's energy fields.

....

The magnificence of the natural world demonstrates that this is a universe of interconnected energy patterns. The glory of nature can be truly awe inspiring. A blood-red sunset, a fabulous beach, that majestic mountain range, a newborn baby, the first snowdrop of spring ... the energy is shimmering and the beauty takes our breath away. The universe is a glorious place and your energy is an integral part of its pattern. Remember this whenever you are feeling low, and go out and look for this sparkling life force; you can find it even in the middle of a city. Look for beauty and you will feel your energy shifting into a higher gear.

We are uplifted every time we cherish and appreciate anything or anybody in our lives. It's so simple we often miss this trick. So next time your heart opens, stay with it and see where this feeling takes you.

Key Points for Contemplation

1 When you are feeling motivated and fascinated no challenge is too great to overcome.

2 The purpose of your life is to realize your full potential.

3 When you make the most of your self you make the most of your life.

4 You can never feel slightly negative or a bit positive: you are either positive or negative, there is no place in between.

5 You can feel glad to be alive – every day.

6 A positive condition is always a magnetic condition and this brings the power of magic into our lives.

7 You are so much more than you think you are: you are a powerhouse of amazing energy.

8 We all seem to carry within us a very damaging inclination to criticize ourselves.

9 Hope opens doors which have been closed.

10 The whole of the energy of the universe is there for us to see if we care to look.

11 Some people can lift our spirits by the power of the energy field which surrounds them.

12 Things are not what they seem.

13 This apparently solid world which we see before us is not at all solid.

14 All matter is energy.

15 Everything is connected.

16 Raise your awareness to raise your energy levels.

17 Universal energy flows through you.

2

The Magic
in Your Life

'Prepare your mind to receive the best

that life has to offer.'

ERNEST HOLMES

Many of us have been living with only an external focus: our only reality has been a material one. The constant quest for material goods has led us to our dissatisfaction: soul food cannot be bought at the supermarket (or anywhere else for that matter). However, this discontent is purposeful because it can open the door to a new way of living (so welcome all those scores below 6 in your Life Zone Checklist). When we are not fulfilling our personal potential we lose direction and purpose and we also start looking around for someone to blame. So if you are into blame at the moment (any person, any institution, the weather, unfairness, the ubiquitous 'them'), you are reading the right book! We are going to do something quite radical: we are going to change our focus from the external (material world) to the internal world of our awareness. We live under an illusion that if we have this sofa, that relationship, a new job, a thin body, that house, this holiday ... we will be happy and contented and peaceful and satisfied. You and I know that this is a short-lived fantasy but we have carried on being material boys and girls because we didn't know any other way to go.

The truth is that we are living in incredibly exciting times of

amazing technological and spiritual awareness. As modern scientific theory endorses the ancient beliefs of mystical tradition
we are now faced with the undeniable truth that *we can change
our outer circumstances by changing our inner awareness.*
This means that, instead of going after something which is *out
there* in the material world, in order to make us feel good inside,
we reverse the procedure. We go *inside* ourselves and change
our awareness and in that way we can attract all that we need to
make us happy.

Because we are all part of the vibrating energy field of our
universe there are some fascinating and interrelated natural laws
which govern the process of life. These principles show how we
are creating the situations and events of our lives by magnetizing people and circumstances with the radiations of our own
personal energy. Figure 3 shows the 4 Principles of Creativity
which follow directly from the knowledge that the universe is
pure energy.

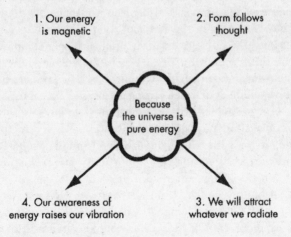

Figure 3 The 4 Principles of Creativity

The 4 Principles of Creativity are

1 Our energy is magnetic
2 Form follows thought
3 We will attract whatever we radiate
5 Our awareness of energy raises our vibration

....

If you apply these principles to your life you will never lose control of your personal reality again; you will always know how to make the very best of every situation, however challenging it might be. Sounds too fantastic to be true? As we examine the Principles of Creativity one at a time, their magical properties will be revealed.

1 Our Energy is Magnetic

We know that atoms are energy fields with positive, negative and neutral charges and that they produce electrical and magnetic forces. Electricity attracts, makes you magnetic and draws things to you. The pole, running from north to south through the centre of the earth, is magnetized, and in exactly the same way the human body is also a magnet. As your fish swim unconsciously in the water of their tank so do we swim unconsciously in our universal sea of electromagnetism. Every time you think a thought it registers in the delicate and sensitive electromagnetism which surrounds us. The laws of attracting and repelling operate electromagnetically. This means that energy of a particular type or vibration is inclined to attract energy of a similar quality and vibration. This principle is operating in your life when: you are 'just thinking about' someone and they call; an amazing opportunity arises 'just at the perfect time'; you hear or read a piece of information which proves absolutely vital ... think of your own examples of this principle. In a negative mood you will dismiss such occurrences as mere coincidence or a random chance. However, there has been much research into this phenomenon of what has been called 'meaningful coincidence' or 'synchronicity'.

Investigation and experience suggest that there is indeed more to this life than a haphazard coming together of events.

Recognizing the Meaningful Nature of Coincidences

The eminent psychologist Carl Jung said that, 'Synchronicity suggests that there is an interconnection or unity of causally unrelated events.' Relax and think about this statement. How do you respond when life presents you with a remarkable set of previously unconnected circumstances which demonstrates to you that everything is clicking into place? Can't remember when it last happened? Think again. Take a particular area of your life and work backwards from where you are now in order to see 'how it all began'. How did you get to meet your partner? What were the circumstances surrounding you getting your current job? How did you come across your present home?

....

When we look at the bigger picture of our lives we can see undeniable evidence of the impeccable timing and synchronicity which give meaning and purpose to our days. In a cynical mood we dismiss such evidence, saying 'it's too good to be true' or 'it's just a coincidence' or 'so what?' and then this powerful moment has gone. The magic lies in being aware of the magnetic qualities of our thoughts and feelings. Evidence of our magnetic powers reveals itself in our daily life, every day. Start looking for this evidence! Look for connections and patterns and meaning in all that is happening to you. As you recognize the synchronicity your life immediately takes on a new dimension: as your awareness develops you increase your magnetizing power. And this is why some people are able to make things happen whilst others are sitting around wondering what's happening. Wake up to the meaning behind the coincidences, signs, flashes of intuition, hunches and dreams which fill your life. Act on this new information and feel your life moving forward at a higher vibration.

2 Form Follows Thought

Thoughts are energy and as you continually think about something you actually draw the energy out from your inner world of thoughts and senses to create that something in the outer world of reality.

Look around you; everything you see was once a thought in someone's head. The building you are in was once an architect's plan; this book began as an inspiring idea; you planned your dinner before you cooked it ... We know that everything is energy and that this energy manifests in different forms to create everything within the universe. Thought, or mind energy is quick, changeable, with a high vibration and so it can occur instantly. We experience between forty and fifty thousand thoughts a day, which just shows how quickly they do appear. Matter is a dense and more compact energy which is much slower to move and change. We can have the thought *I want that fabulous* car immediately, but we can't bring the actual car into our lives at that speed. We can't stand in front of the car, stir up our electromagnetic powers and draw it into our lives; the process takes somewhat longer. Figure 4 shows how it works.

Let's return to that car. Take a look at the following options:

INCREASING LEVEL OF COMMITMENT →

1 I want a new sports car and I keep wishing I had one.

2 I keep thinking about the car and I'm wondering what it would be like to drive.

3 I have decided what make and colour I want.

4 I'm imagining the car sitting in my driveway and I often go to the garage to look at 'my' car in the showroom.

5 I've taken the car out for a test drive and it felt wonderful. It feels as though the car is mine. I'm determined that it will be mine.

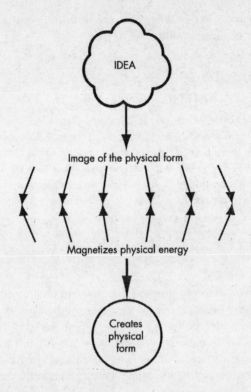

Figure 4 Thought Creates Form

Which option will bring that car into my driveway? Perhaps you think that all of them are fantasies and that 1 is a safe bet because if I stick with wishing I will never be disappointed. Many people wish their lives away and instead of *never* being disappointed they are *forever* disappointed. As I move through the options I increase my level of commitment to the venture. My idea has created a picture which has further developed into a real car which I have actually driven. By the time I have reached option 5 I am actively visualizing living with the car. I will overcome any obstacles to having that car. That car will be mine! *Belief is strong magic.* Think of your idea as a blueprint which creates an image. This image then magnetizes and directs the physical energy so that it flows into its form and eventually materializes in physical reality.

TASK 5

Getting What You Want

Think of a time when you really wanted something; you set about acquiring it and then, eventually it was yours. Remember those positive feelings you had: you could imagine having it; you knew it was within you to get it; you energized your idea and did what you had to do and then you felt the great satisfaction of achieving your outcome. The vital key to getting what you want is always that *you can imagine having it*. Without this belief you won't get what you want, it really is as simple as that.

Now it's pretty easy to imagine that you can create small things that you have done before, for example: cook beans on toast, go to town on a bus, buy a newspaper ... (you see you have been manifesting automatically all your life). When you think about something that you are sure of being able to get you have positive pictures and thoughts, you don't worry about achieving it. You use the following process:

1 You want it.

2 You intend to have it.

3 You are motivated to do whatever it takes to get it.

Become aware of this creative process. This is how you make things happen. Your idea to have something sets up the model of what is to be created. And then, the strength of your emotions (intention, desire, motivation) energizes your thoughts and projects them from your inner world into your outer world. Observe how you create small things because you use exactly the same process to create big things.

THOUGHT ENERGY	X	EMOTIONAL ENERGY	→	MATERIAL ENERGY

3 We Will Attract Whatever We Radiate

Because our energy is magnetic we will attract whatever we radiate. The modern interpretation of this is, 'What goes around, comes around'. We can all remember experiences where we have very clearly reaped what we have sown. I have always been fascinated by this notion and although I have recognized the truth and fairness of it as it has appeared in my life, I have never fully understood the mechanics behind the wisdom until fairly recently.

In practice, this principle demonstrates that all those things we think about most strongly, all those beliefs and expectations we hold and the strength and power of our imagination, come together and attract into our lives exactly what we are giving out. We do indeed attract what we radiate. Think of a difficult time when you were not full of aliveness and energy and recollect the progress of events. When we are faced with great challenges we often become fearful and anxious and this is, of course, a natural reaction. As we become less open to the positive life force we start to feel depressed and our energy levels fall. This negative state tends to attract all the frightening possibilities which are filling our thoughts and so we create a familiar, negative self-fulfilling prophecy: *I told you so, I knew it would all turn out badly; you see, I was right all along.* A dubious achievement and very costly in terms of quality of life. Similarly, when we adopt a positive attitude we radiate expectations of success, happiness and support. I know that this is not always easy to do when we feel trapped in what appears to be an impossible situation, but it really is the only way out. Just think back again to that difficult time when you were low in energy and notice at what point you started to come out of your depression. As soon as you hook into anything positive (however small it might seem) you allow hope back into your life and your energy lifts and everything starts to change.

Remember that sea of universal electromagnetism which you are swimming around in, even as you are reading this? This electromagnetic force is our life force and the more we can absorb, the more 'alive' we will become. We have an incredible 72,000 nerve centres destined for the transmission of electromagnetic forces and we use only about 5,000 of them. This demonstrates the extent of our true potential. Deep breathing, joyfulness, appreciation and relaxation and meditation practices all help us to open more of these energetic points. But the most powerful way for us to access this life force is for us to become aware of its magnificent power. Live it, love it and radiate it and it will flow back to you.

How attractive are you? No need to start thinking about your wrinkles, size of nose, spots, weight, cellulite or any other of the myriad body-image worries we all share. This question is really 'How much electromagnetic energy do you attract?' Are you buzzing with life and crackling with static or are your batteries flat?

'Stickiness' is an interesting Internet concept used to describe the success rate of a web site to attract repeat visitors. If a web site is 'sticky' then it attracts people again and again. Think about your ability to attract the life force (positive energy) into your experiences. If you are open and aware then positivity in all its forms will stick to you repeatedly. If you are closed to your potential then positive feelings, people and situations will drop away from you and you will feel their lack (you will feel negative).

TASK 6

Absorbing the Life Force

Sit quietly and think about your 72,000 nerve centres. If we can use them all we would increase our energy intake by more than fourteen times.

Remember how you feel standing at the sea shore and taking in great lungfuls of air; it's so uplifting and revitalizing, isn't it? So you aren't at the seaside? Well, even if you are at the centre of the metropolis you can still lift your energy and absorb more of the life force by simply becoming conscious of your breathing.

As you take deeper and fuller breaths, feel the changes in your energy. Notice how it feels to be more open and aware. Spend the rest of today remembering your capacity to increase your energy. Visualize those 72,000 points of light shimmering throughout your body; they are there for you to use, so use them. As you absorb the energy of the universe you radiate its positivity and so begin to attract the good things of life. Don't delay, begin today.

4 Our Awareness of Energy Raises Our Vibration

I wonder what images cross your mind when you think of this word 'energy'. Do you see electricity, solar-powered heating systems, someone running on a treadmill or lifting weights, or do you feel the nature of your own energy? Because we know that the universe is dynamic energy we need a new understanding of this word in order to appreciate all its subtle forms.

We use different vibrations of energy throughout our days and when we are operating at a low level of awareness we are probably doing things automatically. Imagine this: you have driven to work in the rush hour and suddenly find yourself 'coming to' when you reach your destination; you were running on autopilot. Now, you park the car and enter your workplace. You still may be too preoccupied to notice the atmosphere as you enter or, alternatively, you might become absolutely 'tuned in' to the energetic vibrations. As you switch from *thinking* to *sensing* you change your awareness and raise the level of your energy. Perhaps you noticed a heaviness and dullness in the atmosphere (not a happy place to work). A pleasant environment is not only about architecture and interior design; the atmosphere depends so much on the thoughts and feelings of the people who use it. We all know how it is to enter a place where you can cut the atmosphere with a knife or which feels cold and unwelcoming. It really is amazing that our personal vibrations have such a profound effect on our environments and yet we often forget to acknowledge the power of this unseen energy. Meanwhile, back at our example, just as your own energy is starting to drop (oh no, another day in this place), a cheery person greets you with a dazzling smile. Up goes your energy as you respond: you feel better already. As you sense your energy lifting you can recognize this heightened vibration and decide to maintain this 'high' all day. This book is full of ideas to help you to lift your own energetic vibrations. You are not at the mercy of a fixed universal reality which operates outside of you and separate from you. Everything and everybody in the universe is connected: there is only one world with two aspects, the visible and the invisible. By learning to appreciate the subtle and 'unseen' levels of energy you can change the nature of the reality which you can see.

Appreciation is a key to the door of awareness. However fed up you feel today, try to make it a day of appreciation. In fact, if you are feeling blue, this task will give even more obvious results as your energy lifts from low to high. Find time to admire the natural world, even if you are in a high-rise office block you can look out of a window and appreciate the beauty of the sky. Our world is a fabulous and radiant place and it's often easy to take the miracle of nature for granted. Look again, and then look again with the eyes of your senses

TASK 7

Feeling the Good Vibrations

Think of your different states of mind as different bands of frequency. When you are depressed, fearful, insecure, low in confidence, unhappy, you are running at a low vibration of energy. Now look at the following words:

Trust	Hope	Thankfulness	Love
Peace	Joy	Harmony	Forgiveness

How did you feel when you read them? The words themselves carry high energetic vibrations, they open our hearts with their meaning and our own energy starts to resonate and harmonize with the energy of the universe. Think of other words which create a similar awareness. Whenever you wish, you can lift your own energy by bringing in these high-frequency bands. Whatever you think will eventually become true for you. Think about gratitude and you will feel grateful; think about contentment and you will feel contented; think about love and you will feel loved.

....

Once we know that our lives form part of an integrated whole we become more purposeful and aware. When we begin to recognize the meaningful nature of coincidences (which we had previously discounted as meaningless) we start to see the bigger picture of our lives. Synchronicity demonstrates that there is significance and intention, a meaning and pattern to all things in our universe: it affirms a divine order of which we are each a part. When we feel our connection with the life force we can trust our intuition and know that our contribution is important. What a way to welcome the day! To wake up in the knowledge that you will attract whatever you radiate is a great motivator for positivity. When we understand how we create situations and magnetize certain people and circumstances with the power of our personal energy, we then know how to take charge of our lives. Even if things are not going so well we know that we can instigate change and start to make new things happen. And, as thought creates form, we can learn how to change our thinking in order to create the world of our dreams.

Key Points for Contemplation

1 We can change our outer circumstances by changing our inner awareness.

2 We swim in a sea of electromagnetism, and this is our life force.

3 The laws of attracting and repelling operate electro-

magnetically. This means that energy of a particular type or vibration is inclined to attract energy of a similar nature.

4 There is so much more to your life than a haphazard coming together of events.

5 As you recognize the meaning, patterns and connections in all that happens to you, your life will immediately take on a new thrust and dimension.

6 The more you open yourself to synchronistic events the more you will become aware of the bigger picture of your life.

7 Wake up to the bigger picture and become a person who can make things happen. Why stay unaware and confused?

8 As you continually think about something you actually draw the energy from your inner world to create that something in the outer world. So beware of what you are thinking!

9 Dreams can come true, but they can't come true if you don't have any. Remember this on a low day.

10 The vital key to getting what you want is that you can imagine having it.

11 We do indeed reap what we sow; check the seeds that you are planting.

12 Become aware of the magnificent power of the life force. Live it, love it and radiate it and it will flow back to you.

13 As soon as you switch from thinking to sensing you change your awareness and raise the level of your energy.

14 Our personal vibrations have a profound effect on our environments. Keep your vibrations high.

15 There is only one world with two aspects, the visible and the invisible.

16 Appreciation is a key to the door of awareness.

17 Our world is a fabulous place and it's often easy to overlook this miracle. Look again, and then look again with the eyes of your senses.

18 Think about happiness and you will feel happy; think about peace and you will feel peaceful; think about love and you will feel loved.

19 High energetic vibrations will open your heart as you harmonize with the energy of the universe.

20 Your contribution is important.

3

The Power of Belief

'You can if you think you can.'

NORMAN VINCENT PEALE

So now we all know why positive thinking works: it attracts good things; increases our energies, creates an upbeat reality, our expectations manifest themselves and it increases our magnetism (all forms of positivity will 'stick' to us). But in spite of knowing all this we still struggle with our negativity. It's so easy to say 'be positive', but sometimes it feels impossible. What if we can't help feeling negative? How do we learn to become positive? Why do some people seem to be naturally more upbeat whilst others carry the world upon their shoulders (even though the world doesn't thank them for it)? Why do we believe the things we do about ourselves, the world and others?

I've just been watching a TV programme where people volunteered to go into an hypnotic trance and then were directed to act in certain ways. A woman was told to stand up every ten seconds and to shout out 'I want my mum'. It was fascinating to watch as she so earnestly called out to her mother, just like a small child. A man was given the job of washing the floor, which he did assiduously, with a mop and bucket of hot soapy water which of course none of us could see. He made such a good job of cleaning the studio floor, moving his 'bucket' and 'mop' carefully around everyone's feet. I'm sure you've seen shows like this; they are highly entertaining and utterly fascinating. How is it possible to get people to do the sorts of things that they would never dream of doing 'normally'? What is this state of normality?

When the man in a trance was cleaning the floor he did so with total conviction; he believed that this was what he was doing and he even created the tools for the job. And then, when he came out of the trance and watched the film of himself with his 'mop' and 'bucket' he was totally amazed and he couldn't believe that he had done such a thing. This man went from a state of *total belief* in his cleaning role to a state of *total disbelief* that he could ever have acted in this way. Such an example demonstrates that belief and disbelief are not set in stone; they are only different types of perception.

Below the Tip of the Iceberg

The human mind has often been likened to an iceberg; the tip which we can see being the conscious mind and the unseen large mass below representing the unconscious (or subconscious) mind. Think of your unconscious as your *underneath* mind. It is indeed underneath your conscious mind and it knows the past, the present and the future. Your conscious mind is the one which thinks and speaks all day long and it can only hold a few ideas at one time. It is critical and analytical and sorts information by focusing on differences. Your conscious mind is non-creative and takes its life from your unconscious. Your underneath mind holds the key to your wisdom, awareness, creativity and flexibility. It regulates your heartbeat and your breathing and all bodily maintenance. Here is your emotional centre and here is stored the amazing multisensory record of all that has happened to you together with all that you have imagined! Some powerhouse of information! Your unconscious works by association: it understands by recognizing similarities.

The famous hypnotist Paul McKenna uses a wonderful metaphor to explain the roles of our conscious and unconscious minds. Imagine a dark room with a variety of objects spread about (the unconscious). A torch (the conscious) can highlight details in the room but can only focus on a few things at once. Whatever the torch shines upon will be lit up and visible and the rest of the room stays dark (although of course it is still there). Similarly, whatever you choose to focus on will be brought to the forefront of your consciousness and all the rest of your multi-sensory information banks remain in the background (but always there, of course).

Each second of our lives our unconscious receives about 2 million messages of sensory awareness, which it sorts out and summarizes before bringing some of them to our conscious attention. Our unconscious is also able to delete any information that our conscious mind can't or doesn't want to handle. Your unconscious mind is your very best friend: it faithfully records each and every one of your words, thoughts and feelings; it never sleeps and will always support you when you are in great need; it always obeys your orders and there are no known limits to its power. Think of a time when you felt that you had come to the very end of your resources, you really hadn't got it in you to go any further ... and then, suddenly, you had the strength, inspiration, courage or whatever was needed. Your conscious mind had come to its finite limit and there was only one place left to go. In desperation it called upon the infinite resources of your unconscious which responded the only way it knows how: creatively, flexibly and magnificently. This powerhouse is yours for the asking, but you must ask.

I expect you have read amazing rescue stories where people performed what seemed to be 'impossible' physical feats. Perhaps you have seen pictures of yogis who have complete mastery over their physical body and can levitate, live without eating or sit naked in the snow for days. These are all examples of the power of the unconscious mind, which can help you do whatever you want to do as long as you believe that you can. The commands to your unconscious must be clear and full of feeling; you must be totally committed and your belief must be 100 per cent. When the chips are absolutely down and, for example, the mother has to lift the car up in order that her child won't be trapped underneath, then disbelief is overridden by desire. She believes that she can lift the car because she has to (there is no alternative) and so her unconscious mind supports her belief and uses all of its resources to save the child. The mother becomes strong enough for long enough to hold up the car so that her child can escape. This is not an act of heroism but rather a fabulous example of the power of the human mind, body and spirit when it is supported by 100 per cent belief. You can if you think you can and you can't if you think you can't!

TASK 8

Your Unconscious at Work

Demonstrate to yourself the power of your own unconscious. Take a troublesome problem which seems impossible to resolve. Remember that nothing is impossible to your unconscious mind, so why not hand it over? Before you go to sleep, bring the problem to mind. Don't start going over and over it in your conscious mind, just imagine it straight in front of you. Now surround it with light. It doesn't matter if you can't see this, it's enough just to know that you are doing it. Now, as soon as you have your package of trouble wrapped up in light, give it to your unconscious. It has gone into your powerhouse where it will be sorted. Let it go and let your unconscious do its work. You don't have to do anything or think anything, the process is continuing unconsciously. Wait in happy expectation for a creative resolution to your dilemma. Know that your problem will be resolved. When the answer comes to you, act upon it immediately. Your unconscious mind will never let you down (unless, of course, you are asking it to).

Let's return for a moment to the man who cleaned the floor so beautifully with his invisible mop and bucket. In a trance state we transcend our rational, conscious, everyday mind. The hypnotist's suggestions go straight to our unconscious mind and, because we can't reason our way out of it with our rational faculties *we have to act as if the suggestions were true.* Stage hypnotists tell people that they are dancers, boxers, weightlifters, singers, and they just act out these roles because they believe that the suggestions are true. Isn't it fascinating to realize that our belief actually creates our reality? Belief is indeed strong magic.

Your Genie of the Lamp

Does your life feel like a perfect fit? Are you the person you most want to be? Is this the life you were born to live? You can have the life of your dreams as long as you can believe your dreams, 100 per cent, no room for doubt. Your unconscious will give you your heart's desire as long as you can give it the right commands. Imagine your unconscious as the genie of the lamp. You rub the magic lamp and the genie appears and says, 'Your wish is my command'. Your personal, magical genie has been answering your commands and doing your bidding since you arrived on the planet. So, you might well ask, why things have gone so wrong? If this powerhouse of information, which is your unconscious, is accessible to you at all times, why are you not living the life of your dreams? Why are you feeling so fed up and dissatisfied? How does it happen that some people get to focus their torch (conscious mind) on positive and successful images whilst others only manage to shine their beam on limitation, unhappiness and negativity. In other words, how does our conscious mind choose what to look at in the powerhouse of our unconscious? Or, to put it yet another way, what orders are you giving your genie?

Programmed for Life

'When we are very little, we learn how to feel about ourselves and about life by the actions of the adults around us.'

LOUISE HAY

And there we have it! We arrive with a clean slate: no critical and comparative faculties, an open door to the power of our unconscious mind; the world is our oyster and we have nothing to prove. We do indeed come trailing clouds of glory. This year we have welcomed two new babies into our family: my granddaughter Alaska and my nephew Daniel. They are so full of love, self-belief and trust; it shines from their eyes and everyone wants to hold them, talk to them and get a smile from them. We were all once like this: fascinated, fascinating, open hearted and just busy being ourselves and enjoying the world. It's good to remember how it all began. Perhaps you can dig out some photographs of yourself as a baby and get a sense of your power and energy at that time. Yes, you were amazing! And yes, you still are!

As you developed and grew from babyhood you absorbed everything that you could. Your trusting and enquiring mind was like a sponge, mopping up anything and everything in its path. A young child below the age of about six cannot rely on its own sense of reason and judgement and so its unconscious mind is busy accepting all things. And this is why, when you were tiny, you unquestioningly absorbed and believed all the messages that were relayed in your environment, whether they were positive, negative, confusing, supporting, alarming, conflicting, joyful, threatening ... In this way we grow up sharing many of the thoughts and behaviour patterns of our parents (who we were watching, and listening to and imitating in our formative years). We internalized these messages, making them part of our own belief system, and so we have unconsciously programmed our minds so that we act, feel and behave in certain ways. This issue of programming is such an important one because it has a determining effect on the quality of our lives. The human mind is like a computer, or rather a computer is like the human mind. We programme a computer as we programme our minds, and, just as 'garbage in, garbage out' aptly describes the relationship between the input and the output of a computer, so it can be applied to the human mind. If our beliefs (what we have put into our minds) are pessimistic and negative then what we give out in our lives will be the same. If our beliefs are upbeat and positive then our thoughts, feelings and behaviours will be a reflection of them. 'Creativity in, creativity out.'

What Do You Think?

The great philosopher and essayist, Ralph Waldo Emerson said: 'A man is largely what he thinks about all day long.' The big question is, what are you thinking about? Let's start with yourself, what sort of person do you think you are?

TASK 9

Your Self-Image

What do you believe to be true about yourself? Read the following list and put the words *I am* before each word. Score as follows: 0 – almost never; 1 – sometimes; 2 – often; 3 – almost always.

rigid	spontaneous	guilty	intuitive	embarrassed
reflective	controlled	sensitive	boring	irritable
worthy	joyful	self-conscious	proud	critical
free	caring	predictable	tolerant	articulate
interesting	depressed	worthless	loveable	adventurous
kind	shy	bossy	negative	lazy
confident	helpless	fearful	capable	flexible
protective	passive	optimistic	happy	temperamental
indecisive	exciting	stupid	self-aware	foolish
cynical	intelligent	trustworthy	supportive	amusing

Look at where you scored 3. What do you think that you are almost always? Make a list. These characteristics are part of your self-image. Now consider the ways that these aspects of your personality affect your satisfaction levels in the various areas of your life. For example, if you thought that you were almost always shy then this could be having a major impact on your social life (you would probably have a low satisfaction score in the friends and love zones of your Life Zone Checklist). Now look at where you scored 0. Make another list of what you believe you are almost never: your self-image does not include these features. Reflect on how the words on this list might be affecting the quality of your life. If, for example, you thought that you were almost never indecisive, then this belief might mean that your assertive behaviour creates high satisfaction levels in your self-image and work zones. Keep your answers to this exercise because we will be referring to it in greater detail in Section 3, Living Dynamically.

Someone once said to me, 'Look, I am what I am and nothing can change that. I've never struck lucky in my life and everything I've done has gone wrong. Why should I believe that anything will ever change for me?' Well, the good news is, we don't have to wait for things to change; we can change our lives by changing the ways we think about ourselves and our world. *Thoughts can be changed!*

A Self-Fulfilling Prophecy

You weave the reality of your life with the threads of your belief, and in Section 3 of the book we will be investigating the exact ways in which you do this. Here we are looking at the process which demonstrates how we perpetuate and reinforce our self-beliefs. By adopting negative or positive beliefs about ourselves we can make our own self-fulfilling prophecy.

Case study

Debbie was in her mid twenties, well educated, unemployed, and living at home when she first became a life coaching client of mine. She was fed up with her life and felt unattractive and unemployable. She had been applying for all sorts of jobs for over a year and, although she had been to plenty of interviews, she was never successful. Debbie had reached the point where she had lost all her confidence and self-belief. Now she dreaded going for interviews, even if the job was interesting. I asked her to run through what had happened at her last interview.

> Well, the job was just what I wanted, working with children with special needs in a unit with lots of good facilities. I had all the qualifications they were asking for and I knew my application form was good. But because I've had such bad luck finding a job I just couldn't believe that I would be good enough at the interview, and I wasn't. I was really nervous before I even got there and when they took all us applicants on a tour of the unit I felt so intimidated. I kept looking at the other candidates and I felt that they looked so much more confident and at ease than me and I just

knew, even before the interview, that I would never get that job. I didn't stand a chance. When I was asked why I thought I would be good at the job I just couldn't answer. When I got the letter to say I'd failed I wasn't upset because I was expecting it.

Debbie had all the qualities needed to do this job, except one: she didn't believe she could do it. If you think you can't do something then it isn't very hard to get others to agree with you. How can someone value your skills if you don't value them yourself? Debbie and I worked on her confidence levels and bit by bit she climbed out of her negative cycle. As she gained more confidence she felt more self-respect and this became very evident. Even her posture improved. Eventually she did get a job she wanted, but only because she felt positive about herself and what she had to offer. Once her expectations changed (*I really think I can do this job well*) her life changed. The interview panel could feel her confident manner and warmed to her and so the interview got better and better. Debbie rang me afterwards and said, *I think I've got it, but even if I haven't I know I've cracked my problem with interviews*. When you can change a negative self-belief to a positive one you can crack anything!

Because our imagination follows our beliefs we constantly find ourselves in cycles which reinforce our beliefs. These cycles work like this: my self-belief is low (I'm no good, can't do anything, bound to lose out ... etc.) and so I paint mental pictures of me being a total failure. These imaginings generate matching emotions (feeling depressed, fed up, unmotivated, unenthusiastic ... etc.), which automatically brings on hormonal changes in my body. These emotional and physical changes affect my behaviour and colour my interpretation of events (I knew that I would fail, I was right all along). Of course a positive belief cycle works in exactly the same way, but will 'prove' that I am a success, as I generate emotional and physical characteristics which reinforce my good feelings about myself. And so it is that my daily life seems to justify what I believe more and more. Thinking positively or negatively has a profound effect throughout your whole being: thoughts affect us emotionally, physically and spiritually. Your mind, body, spirit and emotions are interconnected, so watch your thoughts carefully because they will affect every part of your life. Figure 5, Cycles of Self-Belief, (overleaf), shows how we create our self-fulfilling prophecies. Look at this diagram and think about it in relation to the case study of Debbie. When we first met, Debbie was locked into a negative self-belief cycle. She felt low about herself and so had low expectations of success in the job market (which, incidentally, she blamed on her 'bad luck' at previous interviews). When talking about the job she didn't get, she admitted that her behaviour had been severely affected by her nervousness and lack of confidence. We can never do ourselves justice when we hold back because we think we are not good enough. By the time she was asked why she would be good at the job she had firmly decided that she wouldn't be and so couldn't answer the question. The unhappy episode ended with her accepting her 'failure' (which, of course, she had been expecting all along). But her experience wasn't a failure because it led her to realize that she was creating her own misfortune by her attitude. As soon as we recognize that we are in a negative cycle and there is no one to blame, we have already begun to change. This often happens when we reach rock bottom and it feels like we just can't sink any lower – and then *the only way is up!* So Debbie entered the positive cycle as soon as she decided that she deserved more than she was getting. She had the qualifications and she could do that job as well as anybody else (and probably a lot better). As she learned some simple but effective techniques to increase her confidence her self-respect returned and her expectations changed. Yes, she deserved a good job and she was going to get one (however long it took). And this was an important change in attitude for Debbie; she was not going to let 'failure' stop her. When we hold positive self-beliefs we are strong enough to overcome setbacks and we recognize our 'mistakes' and choose to learn from them rather than be

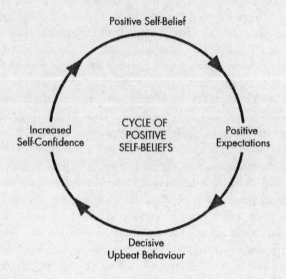

Positive Self-Belief

Increased Self-Confidence

CYCLE OF POSITIVE SELF-BELIEFS

Positive Expectations

Decisive Upbeat Behaviour

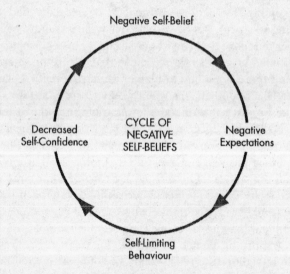

Negative Self-Belief

Decreased Self-Confidence

CYCLE OF NEGATIVE SELF-BELIEFS

Negative Expectations

Self-Limiting Behaviour

Figure 5 Cycles of Self-Belief

defeated by them. Decisive and upbeat behaviour increases confidence, and when Debbie rang to say that she *thought* she had got the job, I *knew* that she had.

Look again at Figure 5 and think about a time when you have been in the depths of negativity or the heights of positivity. What were your differing expectations and how did they affect your behaviour? How did you limit your own behaviour when you were going through the negative cycle? How did you demonstrate your positive feelings when you were upbeat? What happened to shift your awareness from the negative to the positive? We will look at your own personal belief cycles in detail in Sections 2 and 3, but for now just start to become aware of the way these cycles work. If we think we can, then our unconscious (which supports our thoughts at all times) will 'prove' to us that we can. Just believe in yourself. You can!

The Biggest Thought

'When we send a thought out into this substance in which we all live, it sets up waves, and the positive thought is much bigger, giving a quicker tempo, a far greater vibration.'

AL KORAN

As our thought waves radiate from us and attract similar patterns, our beliefs about ourselves and about the rest of the world help to create the type of life that we experience. Al Koran, in his book *Bring Out the Magic in Your Mind,* uses a wonderful analogy to describe the power of positive belief. If we throw a pebble into a pond the ripples will spread out in circles and eventually reach the shore, where they stop. Now, if we throw in two stones at the same time, in different places, and they differ in weight and size, they will both set up ripples or waves which converge on each other. At the point where the two sets meet there is a struggle, as one overcomes the other. The waves of the larger stone sweep over the ripples of the smaller stone. The *bigger* (more positive) your thoughts the more forcefully and powerfully they will swamp the smaller (more negative) ones. Positive thoughts are like the bigger stone, they have the greater impact.

And What Do You Think About the Rest of The World?

Just as we can 'prove' that what we believe about ourselves is true, so we can also ensure that what we think about the world becomes a self-fulfilling prophecy. If we believe that the world offers limited gifts, that there is 'not enough' of anything to go round; that we are here to compete with each other for natural resources and that our universe is dying, then we are indulging in *scarcity consciousness*. This way of thinking works in exactly the same way as negative self-beliefs; small thoughts creating limitation. But hold on there a moment, we really are running out of natural resources, aren't we? Surely it's unreal to believe otherwise? Yes, we do have toxic waste, starving populations, poisoned seas, depleted rainforests and a severely damaged ozone layer, but all these things have only become true for us, because we have believed in scarcity. A feeling of scarcity brings with it greed, aggression and going against the natural laws. Think again and consider this statement: *The universe is abundant: it has everything we need.* This world is naturally prolific: there are no shortages unless we have chosen to create them. There is enough air, unless we decide to pollute it; enough food, if we work with the balance of nature and for the good of all; enough love if we choose to radiate it; there is enough of everything if we believe there is and then act in harmony with those beliefs. If you are still unsure, just start to check out the abundance of the natural world surrounding you: look for abundance everywhere you go. You slice a tomato for a sandwich and notice how many seeds there are inside; just to think that this tomato came from a plant that grew from *one* of these seeds. And how many kilos of tomatoes grew from this one seed? So how many seeds came from the original seed? The maths are staggering: nature never intended us to go short of tomatoes, or of anything else! Notice the number of apples on the tree; tadpoles in the pond; stars in the sky. No, there is no shortage; we have created scarcity, let's create abundance instead.

TASK 10 ....

Your World View

What have you learned to believe about the world and its inhabitants? Put 'I believe that ...' before each of the following statements and answer yes or no. Don't think about which are the 'right' or 'wrong' answers, just go quickly through the list to discover your automatic responses rather than what you think you should say. We are uncovering deeply held and largely unconscious beliefs here, so you might be surprised to discover what you have learned to believe is true.

Yes No

1 Human nature is basically competitive.
2 The more I give the more I will receive.
3 There is never enough of everything to go round.
4 The world is a safe place.
5 Life is a never-ending struggle.
6 We are all connected.
7 The world is full of evil.
8 We have the power to transform the planet.
9 This is a world of plenty.
10 Self-transformation leads to global transformation.
11 Scarcity is an idea which we have created.
12 'Positive thinking' is unrealistic.
13 There is no meaning to life other than to survive.
14 My contribution is important.
15 We create our own reality.

What did you discover from Task 10 about your deeply held beliefs? Is your world a frightening place? Do you live in an abundant universe or are you knee deep in scarcity consciousness? One view of the world allows for the possibility of hope and change whilst the other guarantees that we remain victims. Look for abundance and you will see it everywhere: always hold the *biggest* thought you can, there are no limits except those that we create ourselves. Look for generosity and exuberance and you will attract it, and, as abundance starts to 'stick' to you, the people around you will pick up the vibrations. Consciousness spreads like wildfire, so make sure yours reflects largesse, prosperity, hope and love. As this awareness reaches out to others we will all learn to co-operate because we won't need to compete; we will respect and nurture our resources and we will live in harmony with our environment and with each other. Remember that whatever you believe will come true for you in some way. Make your corner of the world a place of abundance and this awareness will start to affect other people's corners. Self-transformation leads to global transformation; when we change our beliefs we change our behaviour and this is how we change our world. Always hold the biggest thought and sweep aside all idea of limitations. Let go of scarcity and embrace abundance.

TASK 11

Holding the Biggest Thought

Whenever you are suffering with negativity (about yourself, the state of the world or about others), use this simple yet incredibly effective visualization technique. Remember that it doesn't matter if you can't 'see' the images, it's enough to just *know* that they are there. If you are in a private place close your eyes and relax. If you are needing a quick positive fix in the middle of a crowded office, out shopping, or any place where there are people around, you can just do this with your eyes open.

Imagine a pond; perhaps it has bulrushes; maybe you can hear frogs croaking; are there dragonflies swooping across the surface? The sun is shining in a cloudless sky, blue sky. Absorb the details, set the scene and then you can recreate it at any time.

Now see yourself at the edge of the pond, you are looking and feeling confident. You bend down and pick up two smooth grey pebbles, one much larger than the other. As you hold one in each hand you can feel the difference in weight between the two. Notice which hand holds which pebble. Now throw the pebbles into different parts of the pond. As you watch, you see the circle of small ripples made by the lighter stone and the larger circle of ripples made by the heavier stone. You watch as the larger waves overcome the smaller ones and you know that, in just the same way, the positive thought you hold is big enough to overwhelm your smaller and limiting beliefs.

After you have done this visualization a number of times you can eventually reach a stage where you see yourself throwing in only the larger pebble. This action symbolizes your desire to think only the biggest, highest and most positive thought. (There is no need to worry about the exact nature of your biggest thought; it is enough to know that your intention is to go for the thought that creates the biggest wave.)

I use this technique many times a day. Whenever I need an injection of positive energy, I just throw my large, smooth pebble into the pond and know that I have chosen the highest thought (whatever that might turn out to be). Try this technique the next time you need a boost, it only takes a few seconds. Learn to hold the biggest thoughts about yourself and all the people you meet and you will be amazed at the way life starts to treat you.

....

We now know that the quality of our experiences depends absolutely upon the quality of our thoughts. In our very early years, when our unconscious mind was busy unconditionally absorbing all that it encountered, we learned our basic beliefs about the way we are and the way the world is. The amazing truth is that we are not chained to our old thoughts; that *we can change our beliefs* and that this liberates us from our past. If a belief doesn't work for you, then you can change it. If it doesn't do you any good to think very little of yourself then you can learn to appreciate your true worth. If your world is a frightening place and you are limiting yourself with your scarcity consciousness then you can learn to embrace abundance. Imagine your thoughts as the colours in an artist's palette. Beautiful, clear and bright paints can make a dazzling picture, whereas muddy, dull and dreary colours will never radiate on the canvas. Let the canvas be your life and choose the brightest and most beautiful thoughts to create the pictures of your dreams.

Key Points for Contemplation

1 Belief and disbelief are not set in stone; they are only different types of perception.

2 Your unconscious mind holds the key to your wisdom, awareness, creativity and flexibility: it can help you to realize your potential.

3 Desire and motivation can override disbelief.

4 The resources of your unconscious are infinite: the limits of its power are unknown.

5 Belief is the strongest magic of all.

6 You are amazing!

7 Garbage in, garbage out; creativity in, creativity out.

8 Thoughts can be changed.

9 You weave the reality of your life with the threads of your belief.

10 By adopting positive or negative thoughts about ourselves we can make our own self-fulfilling prophecies.

11 Positive thoughts brush everything else aside to reach their objective.

12 The universe is abundant: it has everything we need.

13 There are no limits except those we create ourselves.

14 Consciousness spreads like wildfire so make sure that yours reflects love, hope and prosperity.

15 We have created scarcity, let's decide to create abundance instead.

16 Know that you can always hold the biggest, highest and most creative thought (whatever the circumstances).

17 Fill your mind with beautiful thoughts and your world will become a beautiful place.

18 You can if you think you can!

4

Slug Slime, Trees That Can Smell and Collective Consciousness

> '... *everything in the universe is made up of energy, and this energy creates all the forms and substances of what we call our reality.*'
>
> JAMES REDFIELD

Our physical universe is energy. Think again of the image of our universe as a huge ocean of vibrating energy which creates all forms of existence. This essential energy (the essence of all things) is vibrating at different wavelengths and so creates different forms of matter. All that exists is made of the same basic substance and this energy is always moving; being born, developing and transforming. These movements emanate from one source, from one point, which is the centre of all consciousness. All forms of energy are interrelated and affect each other – we are all connected because we originate from that single point of consciousness. It might be hard to believe that all of nature is aware and conscious, but wait, recent research has confirmed that even slugs are sending messages!

Keep Talking to Your Plants

*'The word vegetable tends to be used
as a term of contempt ... but plants
are not as stupid as people think.'*

PROFESSOR ANTHONY TRAWAVAS

We all know that plants respond to a bit of TLC (tender, loving care) and that they often wilt if they are neglected. But did you know that they respond to environmental information in much the same way that humans do? Professor Trawavas is a leading plant biochemist at Edinburgh University whose research shows that plants do have the capacity for intelligent behaviour. His study of a parasitic vine (called the dodder plant) demonstrates that it only uses its suckers to feed off a host plant if that plant has an 'impressive nutritional value', otherwise it doesn't bother to engage its suckers. The professor concludes that this vine has some way of finding out the information it needs, probably by evaluating the chemicals on the surface of the host plant.

Research at Glasgow University shows that plants contain proteins called cryptochromes and phytochromes that can detect light. Whilst it has been generally accepted in scientific circles that plants actively seek out light, it now seems that these proteins may even allow plants to sense wavelengths *beyond the range of the human eye.* Our definition of intelligence (as the ability to move about and have a brain), could certainly do with an update. US researchers have found that large trees can smell! It was discovered that trees that suffered pest damage were able to 'warn' their neighbour trees to develop protection by giving off smells that the pests found offensive. Other projects show that some plants respond to sound whilst others are able to 'taste' nutrients in the soil and grow towards those fertile areas. Plants, just like everything in the natural kingdom, are endowed with a certain level of awareness: all of nature shares the spark of consciousness.

Smart Slime

My vegetable garden is one of my great joys and although I don't usually have many slugs nibbling away at the produce, they did seem to take more than a passing fancy to my rows of rocket this year. I admit to putting down the dreaded pellets and even to sinking yoghurt cartons of beer into the ground (is this a more pleasurable way to go than dehydration?). But never again will I be able to do this; we will just have to eat our rocket with crinkly edges. How can I, in all conscience, murder a creature that leaves messages for its loved ones to read *in its slime?* A team of researchers at Heriot-Watt University have found that the slime left by slugs contains a 'wealth of information' for other slugs to 'read'. And so slugs are leaving messages to each other in their silvery trails across our lawns and vegetable patches telling of where they are going and goodness only knows what else! Although we still don't know how they read each other's slime, it has become clear that a slug can arrive in the middle of another's trail and know which way it is moving. Computer companies are already showing an interest in 'smart' slime because it's possible that computers could use chemicals in the same way (to relay information) instead of using electronic particles.

And Something Even More Amazing!

Yes, this tale of consciousness becomes even more fantastic. In her brilliant book *Living in the Light* Shakti Gawain refers to a study of wild monkeys in Japan in 1952. These monkeys ate mainly sweet potatoes. One day the scientists noticed that one monkey did something that they hadn't seen any of them do before; she washed her potato before she ate it. This became her habit and soon other monkeys were copying her. Nothing particularly extraordinary about that, you might think. But then, in 1958 when all the monkeys were washing their potatoes before dinner, the scientists on the other islands started to report that their monkeys had also begun to wash their potatoes. No monkeys had been taken from one island to another and there was no physical connection between the islands. And so arose the concept of *the hundredth-monkey syndrome.* This study demonstrated something that is of such great importance, not just for the monkeys but for us humans and the way that we live. When the first monkey washed her potato she introduced a new level of consciousness and when enough monkeys had accepted this awareness it was seemingly 'spread' to the monkeys on the other islands, *even though there had been no direct communication or contact*.

With slugs sending complicated messages to each other, plants sensing wavelengths beyond the human range of perception, trees communicating with other trees and using their sense of smell, some plants responding to sound and even having a sense of taste, and monkeys using telepathy, we must be left wondering about the magnitude of our own human talents. In the evolution of consciousness we are at the very top of the ladder: we are conscious at a mental level and have intellect and the ability to think. If monkeys can share a collective consciousness then what are the implications for our own potential?

Creating a Personal Reality

In the last chapter we saw that our conscious mind was only a tiny part of what we are and know and can be. We are only limited by our beliefs: our unconscious mind, that powerhouse of information is as accessible as we allow it to be. The relationship between our conscious and unconscious mind helps to create our personal reality (whatever we choose to believe about ourselves and the world will come true for us in some way). When we choose to shine our torch of consciousness on something within the darkness which is our unconscious, we become newly aware of that brightly lit 'something'. One way this can happen might be via a revelatory dream. Perhaps you have experienced a new understanding after a meaningful dream: the unconscious often uses the dream state to send messages to our conscious mind. Another way you might have experienced a new awareness is by a feeling of 'suddenly realizing something' that you hadn't realized before. When this happens it's like being hit by a thunderbolt: out of the blue comes the answer and you say to yourself, 'Of course, why didn't I think of that before?' When we really desire to know something our unconscious will always bring it to our attention.

TASK 12 ....

Becoming Conscious

Think back to a time when you had this experience of being jolted into a new awareness. How did this new feeling come to you? Was it through a dream or a sudden realization or did you feel it intuitively? Can you remember how your energy felt? Were you excited and energized by this new information? How did you integrate your new understanding into your life? How did this process change your perspective and your personal reality?

If the new information was hard to assimilate it was probably because you had previously pushed it from your conscious to your unconscious mind. Our unconscious is able to delete information which is painful to accept (we call this denial) and so sometimes becoming conscious requires that we look at old material which has caused us pain in the past. For now, let's just look at how this 'becoming conscious' process works.

- Your conscious mind gets the message from your unconscious mind (via dreams, intuition or 'bolts from the blue').
- You react by feeling more energized (you are incorporating new awareness into your energy field).
- You integrate the new awareness and this changes the way that you perceive your reality.

....

We will look at this process again and again in the following sections because realizing our potential often means that we need to dig deep into our unconscious thought and behaviour patterns in order to shine a light on what is holding us back.

Creating a Shared Reality

But we also share our creation of our reality with others: yes, we are even more sophisticated than the potato-washing monkeys! When those creatures passed on their new habit they did so by using the power of their collective consciousness: we use this power, too. As we swim in our sea of electromagnetism, or consciousness, we can share any of the thoughts, beliefs and awareness that co-exist in that sea. And this is why you can spend the evening with a negative person and feel wretched at the end of it; consciousness is catching (so watch what you choose to share). Meanwhile, back with the monkeys, who demonstrated the truth that every individual contribution counts. The consciousness of every person is linked with the consciousness of everyone else. So, when the heightened awareness of a single person has eventually spread to a significant number (a critical mass) then this new awareness radiates to others via the collective consciousness. This osmosis of consciousness has amazing implications for all of us and for the future of our planet. It is so easy to feel that we have little to offer to the world and that we can make no significant changes because 'it's all too big' and we are just 'too small to count'. This is not true! Everything you think, say or do has great implications: one person can bring about powerful changes just by the power of their own awareness. Think about that first potato-washing monkey. Think about Mahatma Gandhi, who instigated the first non-violent revolution in history. Where fighting had failed, he successfully engaged his people in passive resistance to achieve social reform. His powerful and positive mental attitude changed the consciousness of the Indian people and created a reality of non-violent rebellion.

When a group shares a coherent energy field (i.e. a group of people on the same wavelength with the same intention at the same time), the intensity of the energy is not measured by the number of people but by that number squared. Perhaps some of you have attended workshops, personal development groups or healing circles, or indeed any group which is dedicated to positive change. When such a group meets then you can feel the increased 'charge' of energy in the room. If twenty such people met with a common aim for positive change the power of their dedicated thoughts would magnify by 20 squared – in other words, by a factor of 400.

We Are All Telepathic

*'You are a walking broadcast station,
and you pick up messages constantly
from your community and friends.'*

SANAYA ROMAN

Think of your thoughts as clusters of energy which you send out into the world to become part of the collective pool of consciousness. These *thoughtforms* have a powerful effect on creating both your own personal reality and also that reality which we share with others. We know how our own thoughts attract energy of a similar nature and how this reflects in all areas of our lives. For example, I might be carrying the thought that my relationships are never successful. If my mental pictures tell me that I am 'a boring person', or that I can never be a 'good enough friend', then my unconscious will oblige me by attracting relationships and experiences that confirm my thoughts (remember that we create self-fulfilling prophecies). This very same process works in exactly the same way at the shared level. It's possible to actually 'sense' the thoughtforms of a community of people. Have you ever been in a bar or restaurant and really liked the atmosphere which felt friendly because people were chatting and having a good time? So you go back again and again, becoming part of that upbeat crowd and so helping to reinforce its image as a popular place to go and socialize. On the other hand, perhaps you have visited a place or town where you didn't like the vibes and didn't want to go back. When you go to a party or meet a group of people at work or at leisure you can soon learn to sense the thoughtforms that they share; the atmosphere they create will affect your mood. This is why I am often quoted as saying 'stay away from grumpy people' (I'm quite serious about this).

I'm sure that, like me, you watch TV sometimes and wonder just who wants to watch all the putdowns and gloom that we see on our screens. As more and more people are becoming aware that they have the power to create their own reality, and are not at the mercy of some vast force that is controlling their lives, we begin to change our collective consciousness. As our personal thought broadcasts become inspired with purpose and direction, as we learn to hold the biggest thought about ourselves and the rest of the world, so this energy goes out into the collective pool and inspires other people. This is such a fabulous thing to know, isn't it? Your personal development and growth doesn't just positively affect your own life but it directly affects the people around you by a knock-on effect (enthusiasm, optimism and hope are catching). As more of us learn to live fully, to take responsibility for our lives and to realize our full potential, this telepathic broadcast goes out to others and mass consciousness begins to change. The twenty-first century is inviting us to take responsibility for the state of our planet in the same way that we are learning to take responsibility for ourselves.

TASK 13

Becoming More Telepathic

We communicate in two ways, verbally and non-verbally (telepathically). You are always using telepathy, but you are probably not always conscious that you are doing so. As you become more aware of your telepathic abilities your senses will sharpen and you will pick up even more messages on the broadcast station of your mind.

When you are communicating with anyone today, begin to notice the non-verbal messages that you are picking up. The very best way to become sensitive to telepathic messages from other people is to do something called active listening. The Chinese verb 'to listen' is made up of five characters signifying ear, you, eyes, undivided attention and heart. Apply these five components when you are listening to someone and you will sense so much more than they are telling you. Look for visual clues such as type of eye contact and body language. Notice where words don't match with facial gestures (for example, positive words with a miserable facial expression). Feel the other person's feelings (by opening your heart). This is really easy to do, you just need to practise; their feelings are radiating from them, just allow yourself to catch these radiations. Concentrate on being a listener rather than being a talker; you will be amazed by what you find out with your telepathic antennae.

Everything living shares the divine spark of consciousness and this energy is the creative life force of the universe. Modern scientific research shows that the plant and animal kingdoms have a far greater awareness than many of us had supposed; indeed, all of life demonstrates intelligence to some degree. As we recognize human consciousness as the most highly developed awareness on the evolutionary scale we must also recognize our responsibility to all life forms on the planet. This responsibilty requires our commitment to living and fulfilling our personal potential. For example, when you are working to improve your confidence levels and communication skills your personal development will have an enhanced effect on all those who you meet (and also many who you don't). Consciousness is catching, so raise yours and contribute fully to the collective pool (feel inspired and others will catch that feeling too).

As you bring to light any unconscious thoughts, beliefs and behaviour patterns that create limitation for you, your consciousness will rise and your life will change for the better in every way. You can lift out of scarcity consciousness and all the fear and limitation that it brings. You can embrace the natural abundance and prosperity of the universe and feel the love, hope, optimism, enthusiasm and inspiration that this heightened awareness conveys. As you create new, hopeful and positive realities in your own life so you will contribute to new and harmonious shared realities. When the critical mass of human awareness moves from scarcity consciousness to abundance consciousness we will begin to heal our planet.

Key Points for Contemplation

1 We are all connected because we originate from a single point of consciousness.

2 Everything in the natural kingdom is endowed with a certain level of awareness.

3 Consciousness 'spreads' via the collective pool.

4 When we really desire to know something our unconscious will always bring it to our attention.

5 Your unconscious can speak to you via dreams or flashes of insight or just an intuitive sense of 'knowingness'.

6 When something new enters your consciousness you become more energized (as more awareness enters your energy field).

7 As you integrate new consciousness things will look different and your reality will change.

8 Sometimes, before we can move forward, we need to uncover sensitive or painful memories from the past that we deleted from our conscious minds.

9 As we swim in the vast sea of consciousness we can share any of the thoughts, beliefs and awareness that co-exist in this sea, so watch what you share.

10 Everything you think, say and do has great implications.

11 When a group of people meet who share a coherent energy field, their dedicated positive thoughts are magnified by the square of their number. For example, a thought shared by twenty people would be magnified by a factor of 400.

12 We are all telepathic and we are always picking up messages from the people around us.

13 The quality of our personal reality affects the quality of our shared reality.

14 You can feel someone else's feelings by opening your heart. Just keep practising.

15 You can sense the thoughtforms of a group of people; they create a shared reality.

16 Stay away from grumpy people, unless you want to feel miserable!

17 Consciousness is catching: catch enthusiasm and positivity and let others catch these qualities from you.

18 When the critical mass of human awareness moves out of scarcity consciousness and into abundance consciousness we will start to heal the planet.

19 The divine spark within us can create wonderful and enlightened realities and we are now beginning to realize this.

5

Creative Visualization

'Imagination is more important than knowledge.'

ALBERT EINSTEIN

Only yesterday a client told me that she had been working on her confidence levels, saying positive affirmations and sticking to her action plans and was feeling really great. And then she said, 'I don't know, though, it might all be in my imagination.' Absolutely right, that's exactly where our realities lie. The fact is that we create our experiences by the power and influence of our imagination. This is quite hard to accept because most of us have been taught that our reasoning power guides our lives. We have all heard the maxim, 'Seeing is believing', which is just like saying, 'I'll go in the water once I can swim'. But of course, you can't learn to swim unless you go into the water *first*. Let's turn it round to become, 'Believing is seeing'. And this is how it really works. This isn't a chicken and egg dilemma but a lack of faith dilemma. You can't learn to swim until you go into the water and you can't see something unless you believe it first!

IMAGINATION → MENTAL → BELIEFS → REALITIES
CREATES PICTURES SUPPORTS CREATES

Whatever we imagine becomes true for us in some way or another because we *act as if it is*! Because attention is energy, what we imagine begins to happen. Pessimists can always prove their point (people are no good, no one cares about me, I don't stand a chance ... etc.) but then so can optimists (I was born under a lucky star, people are great, I love my life ... etc.). Have you ever noticed that cynics are never winners? If you are waiting for proof of your personal amazingness before you can believe it, then you will wait in vain for ever. Your imagination is the gateway to your creativity and you are creating the story of your life at every moment, including this one. Your life is a work in progress; how is it progressing?

Imagining Something New

'Now I'll give *you* something to believe. I'm just one hundred and one, five months and a day.'
'I can't believe *that!*' said Alice.
'Can't you?' the Queen said in a pitying tone. 'Try again: draw a long breath, and shut your eyes.'
Alice laughed. 'There's no use trying,' she said. 'One *can't* believe in impossible things.'
'I daresay you haven't had much practice,' said the Queen. 'When I was your age, I always did it for half an hour a day. Why, sometimes I've believed as many as six impossible things before breakfast.'

This extract from *Alice Through the Looking Glass* by Lewis Carroll always makes me laugh. I love the way the White Queen speaks so witheringly of Alice's rational approach. The Queen is a great fan of creative visualization and knows that it needs practice. Of course something remains impossible until it becomes possible. Of course you will be dissatisfied with life until you become satisfied. The key to changing the seemingly impossible into the possible is by changing your mental images. Your imagination is utterly powerful, it supports and endorses all of your beliefs. What sort of life have you visualized for yourself? Do the pictures in your mind create success, peace, confidence and fulfilment or do they create less than this? Perhaps it's hard to believe that circumstances, people and events are attracted to you by your mental pictures and your beliefs. Think back to

The 4 Principles of Creativity which we looked at in Chapter 2. They state that:

1 Our energy is magnetic

2 Form follows thought

3 We will attract whatever we radiate

4 Our awareness of energy raises our vibration

These interrelated principles are based on the knowledge that our universe is pure energy and so we create our own realities with the beliefs and pictures that we hold in our mind. Creative visualization is the technique whereby you use your imagination to create whatever you want in your life. Sounds like magic? Well indeed it is. Hard to believe it can work? It's been working for you all your life. Our natural power of imagination is the basic creative energy of the universe and we are constantly using it even if we are unaware of its power. Many of us have been using creative visualization in an unconscious way (expecting, imagining and creating scarcity and problems). Why not learn to use this fabulous tool in a more conscious way to bring whatever it is you want into your life?

Getting in Touch with Your Imagination

Your imagination is your mental ability to form images or concepts of external objects which are not present to the senses. Maybe you think that you are not a very imaginative person. Close your eyes and think of an orange. What did you see? Did you see its colour, its shape, the texture of its skin? Maybe you 'smelt' it or even 'tasted' it. When we remember our childhood Christmases, what a crowd of images come to fill our senses. Now imagine eating a piece of lemon. Did this raise the juices in your mouth? You see, you have got a very active imagination! Of course, to see imagination at its outrageous best we only need to watch small children at play. Long after the toy has become boring the box still survives as a car, doll's house or bed for a fluffy toy animal. My children used to love dressing up when they were small and as soon as they put on the special clothes they were straight into the role – fairies, soldiers, robots, creatures from space – and a new reality was created. As we grow up and put away childish things we tend to neglect our imaginative powers. When we can't believe in Father Christmas any more and we are just too big to see the fairies at the bottom of the garden our world starts to become a much more rational place. If we have been brought up to be practical rather than creative, and to see daydreaming as waste of time, we will probably need to get our imaginative muscle back into shape. And that's all it takes, a bit of a regular workout!

A Whole Brain

Creative visualization happens in our brain: it's here that we create images. Our brains have two hemispheres, the left and the right. Figure 6 shows the way that the functions of our brain are divided.

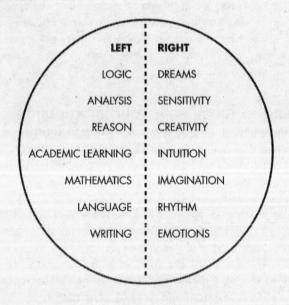

LEFT	RIGHT
LOGIC	DREAMS
ANALYSIS	SENSITIVITY
REASON	CREATIVITY
ACADEMIC LEARNING	INTUITION
MATHEMATICS	IMAGINATION
LANGUAGE	RHYTHM
WRITING	EMOTIONS

Figure 6 The Two Sides of the Brain

Research has shown that the left brain is connected to the right side of the body and it specializes in logic, analytical reasoning or thinking. It can only cope with one thing at a time and it processes information in a linear way. It focuses on memory and recognition of numbers or words. This side of the brain is very important for scientists, writers and mathematicians. Here lies the seat of reason. The right brain is connected to the left side of the body and specializes in intuition and holistic thinking. It can cope with many simultaneous inputs and can process in a non-linear way and it focuses on memory and recognition of people, places and objects. This side of the brain is obviously very important to artists and other creative people. It dictates our spatial awareness; body consciousness; musical and artistic ability and is the seat of our dreams and passion!

When you look at the diagram you will see how most of us have been taught to be left-brained rather than right. Of course, nature in her wisdom endowed us with the qualities of reason and rationality *as well as* the power of our imagination and intuition. We were perfectly designed. Be assured, there has been no mistake, you have all the qualities you need for faultless functioning. We need desire and imagination (right brain function) to visualize creatively our new, dynamic realities, and we need reason and practicality (left brain function) to activate them. If you believe that you are 'not a creative person', then you are in the majority. Most of us have concentrated on left brain development (and so feel a bit rusty in the creative department). You will see how easy it is to tap into your right brain and discover the magnitude and extent of your creative potential. You have all the qualities you need to create a magnificent life.

Going to Alpha Level

Imagine the ocean with its waves pounding continually and rhythmically against the shore. All things have a pulse and a rhythm just like the sea: light and sound form waves and every colour we see and every sound we hear has its unique frequency and vibration. Your body works as a rhythmic, pulsating organism and your brain produces waves which change according to your state. When you are awake and engaged in worldly activity your brain is engaged at the beta level (this is the level you are at now as you read this page). Brain activity increases under stress and this heightened frequency makes us feel even worse (we all know what this is like). Everything that passes through your mind plays a part in creating the rhythm of your brain waves and daily pressure just helps to increase the frequencies. But when we are asleep our brains engage in the alpha level of awareness, here the frequency is lower and we are relaxed. It is possible to change the frequency of our brain waves from beta to alpha whilst remaining awake and conscious, by participating in aerobic activity, for example (which is why so many people go the gym or for a run to 'clear their heads'). In the lower frequency alpha state we feel well, focused, clearer and calmer. However, we don't have to get physical to change the state of our mind. If we relax and slow down our breathing we can also achieve this condition, and activities such as yoga, t'ai chi and meditation can also take us from beta to alpha. In the alpha state we are able to let down any personal barriers which are stopping us accessing the imaginative and creative skills of our left brain (such as beliefs about 'having no imagination' and 'not being creative', etc.). Alpha waves are characterized by their creative nature. Have you ever become completely absorbed by a project so that time has flown or stood still for you? Have you ever been overwhelmed by a natural scene and felt a part of the connecting web of all things? Has your heart ever been touched by the power of your emotion? Did you ever feel so happy that you could just 'jump for joy'? These are all times when you would have been at the alpha level, when both hemispheres of your brain were in absolute harmony and the creative energy of the universe was harmoniously flowing through you. When we use the technique of creative visualization we go to the alpha level of awareness, and in this state we free our imagination and free our minds.

Getting Into a State of Relaxation

We can easily reach the alpha level by going into a focused and relaxed state of awareness. This is a wonderful exercise which you can do at any time (whether you are actively visualizing something or not). Please don't ignore this task – it might be the most important one for you in the whole book.

Find a quiet place where you will be undisturbed for a few minutes. Sit comfortably and become aware of your breathing. As the numerous thoughts start to occupy your mind, just notice them and then take no notice of them (the mind never stops chatting). As you follow your breathing become aware of your body. When you are ready, imagine that your whole body is relaxing. Start with your toes and feel a wave of relaxation and calm enveloping your feet, calves and thighs. Your legs begin to feel heavier. Now bring this feeling of calm and relaxation up into your abdomen and lower back and then into your chest, upper back and shoulders. Let your shoulders drop. Your body is feeling very heavy, warm, peaceful and relaxed. Now, let go of all tension in your hands, arms, neck, head and face. Feel your facial muscles letting go and your jaws and eyes relaxing. When you are comfortable and at ease notice a feeling of peace and serenity. Enjoy! When you are ready, just open your eyes and rub your hands together and give yourself a few moments to acclimatize to the world again.

....

We shall return to this exercise many times and you will become used to going into this state of relaxation. At first you will have to read the directions as you do the task but soon you will be able to do it very easily and quickly. When you are familiar with the instructions, close your eyes throughout the exercise to get maximum benefit. In future, whenever I ask you to get into a 'relaxed state', I will be referring to this technique.

Starting to Visualize

Many people are worried by the word 'visualization': they are sure that they can't 'see' things the way they are meant to; can't tap into their imagination; won't be able to do it 'properly'. If this is you then just relax. First, remember that you are always using the process of creative visualization but usually in an unconscious way. The only difference now is that you are going to become conscious of your mental pictures so that you can change them to improve the quality of your life. So if you feel that you can't 'see' anything it really doesn't matter; we all use our imagination in different ways. You may experience visualization as a feeling or impression, or even a knowingness. Try this quick experiment to check the way that you perceive mental images.

Close your eyes and think about a very familiar place, perhaps a well-known room. 'See' the room in your mind's eye. Look at the furniture, notice the colours, look for the details. Build up an image of your room. Now, imagine walking into the room and closing the door behind you. Pick up a well-known object, touch the curtains, sit in a chair, put yourself in the picture. Now open your eyes. You have just been visualizing; do you see how easy it was?

Now close your eyes again and think about a happy occasion. Bring back the positive emotions that you felt at the time. See yourself as you were then, delighted, excited, happy ... Now open your eyes. There, you've been visualizing again ...

Creative visualization comes to us naturally. It's as easy as breathing, but just like breathing it is usually an unconscious activity. You are about to learn how to consciously create whatever you are looking for in your life. Have no doubt about your ability to do this, you are a natural! The following five-step plan gives important general guidelines to effective visualization. Don't get too bothered about the details here, we will go back to these steps again and again as we deal with your own personal visualizations in the following sections of the book.

Five Steps to Successful Creative Visualization

1 Choosing your goal

Think about your life zones (see page 2) and choose something that you would like from any of these areas. It might involve your self-image (perhaps you would like more confidence), or you might want a job change, or improved relationships, or more money. Whatever you decide to go for must be something that you feel is attainable in the short term. Don't go for long-term goals at the moment until you have really got used to using the process. Go for something that only feels marginally out of your reach and you will experience success very soon which will encourage your progress towards greater goals. In other words, choose something that you really believe you can achieve. Write down your goal (very important!).

2 Making the picture clear

Now, *see* your goal being realized. Get into a relaxed state and imagine achieving your goal. See, feel, experience yourself feeling confident and successful, enjoying a fabulous new relationship, job, car or whatever. Put yourself at the centre of the scene and make the picture come alive, feel the energy of this new happening, get excited and see it *occurring now*. You must see it happening already because if you wish for it in the future it will always stay there (just ahead of you, always out of reach). The reason for this is that our unconscious mind obeys our conscious directions to the absolute letter. So if you visualize that wonderful new house in the future, that's exactly where it will stay. This may be an extremely important point for you: if you are not visualizing it *already happening, in the present*, then your visualization cannot happen, however much you try.

3 Focusing on the images of everyday life

Let the pictures of your idea into your daily reality. Do this by
bringing them to mind as you go about your daily business as
well as during active creative visualization periods. So, as you
are driving along, see your new success happening. As you
push the trolley around the supermarket see that fabulous new
house. Waiting for a bus? Drift into a reverie about that
wonderful new relationship. You will be amazed by the amount
of time that is available for visualizing. As you get into the
habit it will start to grow on you. Be assured that if you are *not*
using your mind for active creativity, it will fill itself with all
sorts of unconscious negative nonsense (and we all know what
that attracts). Light daydreaming and reflection are attributes
of alpha awareness and this state provides the optimum
conditions for successful visualization (and it makes you feel
terrific). Keep your wonderful, positive images alive
throughout the day and they will soon start to become a part of
your reality.

4 Energizing your goal

Support your pictures with the appropriate thoughts. We know
how beliefs and images are so closely interrelated. If I am
visualizing a successful outcome in some area of my life but am
running with a contradictory belief (for example, that I am
always a loser) then my visualization cannot come true.
Effective visualization involves images and thoughts that
match each other. When we are bringing change into our lives
we need to support our new, vibrant mental images with
powerful and encouraging positive statements. In the example
given I would need to create a new belief to endorse my image
of success; I could affirm that 'I am a winner'. Positive
affirmations play a vital part in the process of creative
visualization. These affirmations often appear to contradict our
true beliefs (and in fact that is exactly how they work, by
replacing old negative thought patterns). We will be looking at
your own personal affirmations to see how they are helping or
hindering you in the next section, Transforming Your Life. For

now it's enough to know that affirmations (thought patterns) and visualizations (mental pictures) *must* match for the magic to work.

5 Appreciating whatever happens

Remain aware of what you are trying to achieve and notice what is happening. Things are always in a state of flux and sometimes our ideas and goals change. If this happens, make sure you acknowledge it otherwise you might feel that you have failed in some way or that the process doesn't work. If your visualization loses its initial appeal then your desires and needs have changed. Recognize this, let go and move on. And if you *don't* change your mind and you *do* stick to the process you will definitely reach your goal. When this happens it's so easy to miss it. You know that phrase, 'moving the goalposts'; well, it's very easy to do. It seems impossible at the moment to imagine missing the point when you score your goal (achieve the objective that you are working towards). But this happens over and over again because as we move closer and closer to the fulfilment of our plan it begins to look less and less like the wonderful achievement that it is. Remember that one of the principles of creativity is that *our awareness of energy raises our vibration.* The key to this heightened awareness is appreciation and it is vital that we remember to appreciate and give thanks for the realization of our goals. This appreciation feeds and enhances our creative power as we recognize that we have indeed created a new reality. Respect your creativity, it truly is your genie of the lamp.

It is time now to move out of theorizing and into practising. The rest of the book is a practical application of all the things we have discussed so far. There will be plenty of opportunity to learn how to use the techniques effectively, but for now let's just give the process a go and begin to stretch the wings of our imagination.

Creating a New Reality

Choose your goal and write it down (this physical action helps to make it real). Make sure that you believe that your objective is achievable in the fairly near future (don't try long-term aspirations until you are confident in the process). Go into a state of relaxation and tune into your imagination. See your wish come true. Put yourself at the very centre of the scene, see the detail, hear the sound, feel the appropriate emotions, tap into the heightened energy, bring the setting alive and make it feel real: live the dream now. When you feel the 'aliveness' recede, the visualization has ended. Return slowly from this different state of awareness, rub your hands together, open your eyes and come back into yourself. Focus on your new pictures throughout the day and let the new reality become a part of your everyday consciousness. Remember to energize your goal with strong and appropriate positive affirmations (*I am a success; I am confident; I have a terrific new job; I own my dream car; my relationships support me; I am healthy; I love my life ...*).

Do this for a week, giving at least fifteen minutes a day to your relaxed-state visualization. Support this by daily focus as you go about your business and ensure that your thoughts (affirmations) match your pictures. Reflect upon your situation at the end of the week. What has changed? Look carefully with your inner eyes, the change might be subtle but it will be there.

....

You are beginning to open your imagination to the infinite possibilities that your life offers you. Embrace this chance to make the most of yourself and you will indeed be able to transform your life.

Key Points for Contemplation

1 We create our experiences by the power and influence of our imagination.

2 Believing is seeing.

3 Attention is energy, so what you imagine begins to happen.

4 Cynics are never winners.

5 Your life is a creative work in progress and you are the artist.

6 Things always remain impossible until they become possible.

7 Creative visualization is the technique whereby you use your imagination to create whatever you want in your life.

8 We need *desire* and *imagination* (right brain function) to creatively visualize our new, dynamic realities, and we need *reason* and *practicality* (left brain function) to activate them.

9 Alpha waves are characterized by their creative nature and when we are using creative visualization we go to this alpha level of awareness.

10 Creative visualization comes to us naturally and is as easy as breathing: we have been visualizing (unconsciously) all of our lives.

11 You may not 'see' anything when you visualize, you may instead experience a feeling or impression or an awareness.

12 You must believe that you can achieve your goal or the visualization will not work.

13 When you imagine yourself achieving your goal you must visualize it already happening, in the present. If you imagine it happening in the future it will always stay there.

14 Allow the pictures of your new reality to enter your daily life, by focusing on the images throughout the day.

15 If you don't consciously fill your mind with active creative thought it will fill itself with unconscious negative nonsense.

16 Positive affirmations play a vital part in the creative visualization process. Our thought patterns and mental pictures must match for the magic to work.

17 Everything is in a state of flux and sometimes our ideas and goals change. Be prepared to recognize if this happens to you and remain flexible.

18 Check that you are not moving the goalposts.

19 Always appreciate and give thanks for the realization of your goals, this will enhance your creative power.

20 Respect your creativity, it is your genie of the lamp.

21 Stretch the wings of your imagination and open to the infinite possibilities that your life offers you.

Transforming
Your Life

What Sort of Realities Are You Creating?

'Find yourself and be yourself: remember, there is no one else on earth like you.'

DALE CARNEGIE

Whenever we are feeling unfulfilled and dissatisfied with our lot it is a sign that we have grown out of our lives; somehow, they just don't fit us any more. The world is moving and changing at every moment, and so are we, but sometimes it's hard to remember this. Perhaps one day you find yourself looking around your workplace and thinking 'It's time I moved on'; or maybe your social circle starts to feel small and limiting; you might be affected by meeting someone new who is full of fresh ideas and aspirations and your own horizons begin to look constricting; your love life might lose its lustre; you may just feel low and miserable a lot of the time. Rather than seeing this discontent as a bad sign, recognize it as a signal to you that it's time to change something. If you grew out of a piece of clothing or it became too threadbare to wear, you would buy something new. But sometimes we find it so hard to recognize when we outgrow relationships or situations or self-expectations, and so we continue in our old ways, becoming more and more dissatisfied and bored.

Being Yourself

When the vision of who you are doesn't fit with the vision of who you want to be then you are no longer being true to yourself. It's then time to find the new you. You will need to ask yourself some searching questions, such as What isn't working for me any more? How can I improve the quality of my life? Would I like to see changes in certain relationships? Are there things that I have never done that I would love to do? Why are there problems in some areas of my life?

Don't worry, the world won't fall apart if you dare to ask yourself such questions; there's no risk involved when you are being honest with yourself. You don't even need to try to work out the answers, just become aware of your need for change. Sometimes we can struggle for years being an ugly duckling (always feeling left out and different) when in fact all along we were an entirely different species of bird. Over the years I have heard so many stories from people who have created a lifestyle which doesn't suit them. They often describe themselves as 'failures' and feel that life has delivered them a cruel blow. It can be hard to accept that we are responsible for the lives we make, especially when we are feeling unhappy, discontented and dissatisfied.

Case study

Maria is in her early forties, was married for twenty years and is now divorced. She was brought up in the countryside, where her father was head gardener of a country house with a large estate. Her parents were poor and were determined that their daughter would have the very best education so that she could make a go of her life. Maria was bright and her parents made financial sacrifices so that she could go to university. After gaining a degree in modern languages she trained for another year so that she could teach and then took up a post in a London comprehensive. She married another teacher and spent nearly twenty years teaching.

I hated it, even at the beginning. I wasn't a 'natural' teacher and I never felt the dedication that so many of the staff obviously did. My husband, Tom, was born to teach and he loved every moment of his job. Even after a long day he was enthusiastic and motivated by his work and I began to feel like a total failure. I became a dull person who never could seem to get inspired by anything and I was terrified of having children of my own. It's hard to believe that I put myself through such agony for almost twenty years, but I never questioned why I was doing a job I hated; I just kept going. My parents had given up so much for me, I was their dream come true and I knew how proud they were. And then Dad died, which was a great blow, and I started to get very emotional about everything. Tom and I were also coming to the end of the line. Our relationship was never a joyous one, he was so involved with his vocation and I was pretty depressing company. He met another woman just after my father's death, and I was relieved when he moved out. It was just like the end of a whole lifetime of being someone who wasn't me. I felt fabulously free to do what I wanted and I signed up for night classes in reflexology, aromatherapy and massage. I was fascinated by alternative therapies and suddenly my life came alive. I left my job, carried on with more training courses and now run my own alternative therapy practice in a small market town. I have made a new life for myself and I know now that I can be happy. For all those years I was just living out someone else's dream which wasn't my own, and now I feel that I have come back to myself.

Maria had spent many years pretending to be someone she was not, and when she realized that it wasn't her fault that she was so unhappy she was able to make new decisions and choices which changed her reality. You must have heard that saying 'we make our own bed and have to lie in it'. Well it's true, in part. We definitely make our own bed, but if it's uncomfortable we are actually quite free to go off and make a new bed (metaphorically speaking, of course). Take a look at your life, is it too uncomfortable for you?

Are You Being Victimized?

This might sound like an odd question as it brings to mind issues such as bullying, hate mail, even physical violence. But we can become a victim to others in many subtle as well as not so subtle ways. Unwittingly, we can live our lives the way we do because of other people and unless we are continually checking out our feelings about 'why we do the things we do', we will remain in blissful ignorance of our victim status. When do you stop being a good friend and start to become a victim? When do you stop becoming a good parent and slip into being victimized by your children? Where is that point when your conscientiousness at work becomes burdensome to you and you feel taken for granted? These are tricky questions, aren't they? We are in subtle realms here: we are asking where do our needs end and another's begin. Perhaps you feel that you know your boundaries, that is, how far you will go for others. Maybe you can easily say, 'Yes, I will go this far and no further.' But I think that we are all always juggling with the balls of potential victimization. Remember that everything changes; relationships change and people's needs change. For example, a friend might be in trouble and desperately wants to talk to you. Of course you meet and listen to his problems, even though you had a dinner date already fixed. You come away feeling that you have done a good job, been a friend in need, and all in all it doesn't seem to matter about your lost evening. And then he calls again in desperation and you don't feel quite so philanthropic. If this continued you would no doubt have to put a stop to it; but when and how? When would you decide that your needs came before his? When and where would you draw your line in the sand? For all of you who are parents I hardly need to continue; I know that you know all about the invisible line that exists between being dedicated to the well-being of your child and being totally taken for a ride! The clue to the answer to the question, 'Am I being victimized here?' lies in your feelings. If you are feeling guilty, irritated, low in self-esteem, impatient or muddled and confused around a particular person and/or situation, then you are allowing yourself to be victimized.

A victim is a person who gives away her power to other people. She is unconsciously creating realities in her life (relationships, experiences, situations, dilemmas) which reflect her negative beliefs, and she blames her discontent on others; she is a loser. A non-victim knows that she is responsible for the quality of her own life; she maintains a positive outlook and thereby attracts the best possible circumstances, relationships and lifestyle. She consciously creates her life by using positive affirmations and visualizations: *she has the power and so she is a winner!*

Think about your victim status over the next few days. Don't get wound up about it (this increases your capacity to be victimized), just start noticing the places where you are less than happy to do what you are being asked to do. We will come back to this later, to see how our potential to be victimized can be swept aside by the magnificent power of our creative consciousness. Yes, that indecisive and worried part of you that just can't say 'no', *can be transformed*. It's easy to become one of those people who can stand up for themselves; it's easy to create new realities. The question is, how much do you want to change? Think about this.

You wouldn't have bought this book unless you had felt the need for changes in your life. And so now it's time to get down to the real nitty gritty, the reason that keeps you reading. Let's begin to take a look at your own individual lifestyle. *Just Do It Now!* is a practical book and you are about to put into practice all the things that we have been looking at so far. For this you will need to start a personal journal, so go out and buy an attractive notebook for this purpose. Now check your scores on the Life Zone Checklist on page 2. What were your satisfaction level scores in each of your life zones: Self-Image, Love, Family, Friends, Health and Fitness, Money, Work? Make a note of them in your journal because you will need them in the next task.

Assessing Your Life Zones

This assessment looks at who you are and where you are going right now in your life. Put all your answers into your journal, let's see it all in black and white, no dressing it up, just stick to the facts. Your present satisfaction level is the number you scored in your Life Zone Checklist.

Self-Image

My present satisfaction level is . . . .

I am happy/unhappy with this score . . . .

The words I use to describe myself are . . . .

When I reflect on my self-image I feel . . . .

I believe that I am . . . .

My hopes and fears about the way I see myself are . . . .

Love

My present satisfaction level is . . . .

I am happy/unhappy with this score . . . .

I would describe my love life as . . . .

When I think about my intimate relationships I feel . . . .

I believe that love is . . . .

My hopes and fears about intimacy are . . . .

Family

You might need to answer separately for different family members. If you are having difficulties with anyone there will probably be a lot to write. Don't get stuck in emotions here, just answer as factually as possible and then move on to the next question.

My present satisfaction level is . . . .

I am happy/unhappy with this score . . . .

I would describe my relationships with the members of my family

as . . . .

When I think about the members of my family I feel . . . .

I believe that families are . . . .

My hopes and fears for my family relationships are . . . .

Friends

My present satisfaction level is . . . .

I am happy/unhappy with this score . . . .

I would describe my social life as . . . .

When I think about my friendships I feel . . . .

I believe that friendship is . . . .

My hopes and fears for my friendships are . . . .

Health and Fitness
My present satisfaction level is . . . .

I am happy/unhappy with this score . . . .

I would describe my health and fitness levels as . . . .

When I think about my levels of health and fitness I feel . . . .

I believe that being fit and healthy is . . . .

My hopes and fears for my state of fitness and health are . . . . . .

. . . .

Money

My present satisfaction level is . . . .

I am happy/unhappy with this score . . . .

I would describe my money situation as . . . .

When I think about money I feel . . . .

I believe that money is . . . .

My hopes and fears about money are . . . .

Work

My present satisfaction level is . . . .

I am happy/unhappy with this score . . . .

I would describe my working life as . . . .

When I think about the work I do I feel . . . .

I believe that work is . . . .

My hopes and fears for my working life are . . . .

Taking Charge of Your Life

What was it like answering these questions? If your satisfaction level, taken from you Life Zone Checklist, fell below 6 for any of your life zones, you have crossed the line from positivity into negativity. Remember the basic truth, that everything in the universe is made of magnetic energy and thus we attract whatever we radiate and whatever we keep thinking about will eventually come true for us. So what are you attracting into your life? Look at your answers, look particularly at where your satisfaction level lies below 6 (below the positive/negative line). If you are experiencing negativity then you must be giving it out in some way (we magnetize whatever we radiate). Yes, the buck stops here, with you. And what a relief that is! If there really was anyone else to blame for your predicaments you would be absolutely stuck until they decided to change things. But your life is in your own hands, so get a grip and take charge of the proceedings.

Notice your feelings and beliefs about each life zone. Now let's take at look at Love (always a good place to start). This is an extract from a personal journal of a client whom we shall call Jo. Here she assesses her love life by answering the questions that you have just completed.

My present satisfaction level is ... 4

I am happy/unhappy with this score ... unhappy

I would describe my love life as ... unpredictable, up and down, unreliable.

When I think about my intimate relationships I feel ... that I am not supported enough and that all my relationships eventually fail because my partners will never commit themselves to me or show me how they are feeling.

I believe that love is ... a fantasy which never delivers the goods.

My hopes and fears about intimacy are ... I hope that I will meet someone who is just for me. I fear getting too close to someone in case they let me down.

Now take a look at Jo's answers. Obviously we have no background information and only a few words to go on, but they can tell us quite a lot. Examine them in the light of what you know about how the power of our beliefs creates our own personal realities. What is she *really* looking for and what are her beliefs about love? Can you see any patterns here? She seems to have got herself into a negative loop where her expectations are delivered time and time again ('my partners will never commit to me or show me how they are feeling'). This loop is a pattern which is based on beliefs and experiences which have made her afraid to get too close to anyone. Yes, Jo is getting just what she wants: she is afraid of intimacy and so she makes sure that she attracts men who can't or won't give it. Our thought, emotional and behaviour patterns are our own personal arrangements of energy which clearly radiate from us into the universe. They send out their own specific and unique messages and their matching patterns are magnetized to them. Think of it as finding a matching glove which makes the pair. It's so neat, isn't it? We really do get what we give. We need to be able to check our energy patterns so that we can know *exactly* what we are inviting into our lives.

So, although we don't know much about Jo, we can look at her beliefs and feelings and hopes and fears and discover certain thought and behaviour patterns. It's so much easier to recognize other people's patterns than to recognize our own (and I should know!). In spite of this, and bearing in mind what we know about the way that energy creates its own self-fulfilling prophecy, take another look at your own answers to Assessing Your Life Zones. Do you notice any repeating beliefs and feelings? Is there an underlying feeling of negativity or positivity? Can you get a sense of some of your own patterns and how they are helping to shape your life? Don't worry if nothing is coming clear yet, it will. We are going to put your patterns under a magnifying glass and all the bits will be revealed (but only to you, of course). Once you are aware of the ways that the power of your thoughts, beliefs and behaviour are creating your experiences you can then make decisions about what is working for you and what isn't. And then, *you can create new realities!*

Key Points for Contemplation

1 Everything changes, including us, but sometimes this is hard to accept.

2 When who you are doesn't fit with who you want to be then you are no longer being true to yourself.

3 You are never at risk when you are being honest with yourself; risk lies with dishonesty and denial.

4 You might be under an illusion that you are an ugly duckling when in fact you are a beautiful baby swan!

5 We might make our own bed but we don't have to lie on it if we don't want to: we are always free to make a new and more attractive and comfortable bed.

6 Take a good look at your life; is it getting too uncomfortable for you?

7 We are always juggling with the balls of potential victimization.

8 When you are wondering if you are being treated like a doormat ask yourself, 'How am I feeling?' If you are muddled, low in self-esteem, guilty or irritated (or all of these) then you are acting the victim.

9 A victim is a loser who gives her power away to other people.

10 A winner accepts the responsibility for the quality of her life and she keeps her power.

11 Ask yourself, 'How much do I want to change?'

12 If you are experiencing negativity then you must be giving it out in some way.

13 Your life is in your own hands, so decide to get a grip and take charge.

14 Our thought, emotional and behaviour patterns are our own personal arrangements of energy which clearly radiate from us out into the universe, where they find their exact match.

15 When we know how to check our energy patterns we can find out why our lives are as they are; then we can change our patterns to change our experiences.

16 You have the power!

Overcoming Your Obstacles

*'They must often change
who would be constant in happiness.'*

CONFUCIUS

When you assessed your life zones in the last chapter you reviewed your satisfaction levels. You know whether you were above or below the positive/negative line in each of the zones: you know what you scored and now you can found out *why* you scored it. Why do your relationships become so complicated? Why is it so difficult to maintain a positive self-image? When will you be able to stop worrying about money? Is it possible for you to love the work you do? How come it's so hard to motivate yourself to keep fit and healthy? Of course, some of these issues may not be a problem for you but it's highly likely that you are locked in a negative spiral in some areas of your life. You would be amazed to know how many people struggle to survive all that life seems to throw at them. The great philosopher Henry David Thoreau said that most people live lives of 'quiet desperation', and this is so true. Just take a look around you: look for aliveness, enthusiasm, excitement, interest, motivation, positivity, peace and happiness; how much do you find? The sad fact is that the majority are indeed quietly desperate and so, you see, you are not alone with your problems. We learn and grow and develop as we face the challenges in our life: life is a training course in learning how to live. There is an art to living well and it has nothing to do with quiet desperation and everything to do with understanding some basic principles.

Your Life Is a Training Course

When your mind, body, spirit and emotions are flowing in harmony nothing can hold you back: your life flows smoothly and you feel in tune with the rest of the world. Everyone is looking for this feeling, we all want to feel centred and purposeful and full of enthusiasm. Think of your life as a training course which begins at birth and ends when you leave the planet. The modules of this course come in the form of personal challenges (problems, discontent, relationship hassles ... etc.) and we are here to learn from these modules. If we don't learn from our lessons we have to repeat that part of the course. For example, let's imagine that I am attracted to men who victimize me in some way. The lesson for me is *to recognize* that I keep going for the wrong sort of man, *to understand* why I do this and then *to change* my behaviour. If I don't learn this lesson the module will be repeated (I will fall for the wrong chap again). When I finally grasp this module I will have learned a lot about myself and about the type of man I would like to attract. And so each learning experience brings more awareness and balance into our lives. But there is never an end to the learning and when we have learned something new and assimilated its meaning we move on to the next module. *You are a work in progress.* You are here to learn life's lessons and they will never stop until your life ends. Accept this. Recognize that your life is an ongoing process of self-awareness and that the very nature of life (moving in cycles) ensures that you will continually experience ups and downs.

Looking for the Opportunity

There is no 'happily ever after' in the sense that you will never face challenges again: your challenges ensure that you reach inside yourself and rise to your highest potential. The Chinese word for 'crisis' is the same as the word for 'opportunity'. Think about this. When did you last face a crisis? Where did the hidden opportunity lie? Did you take this chance to learn more about yourself? It is usually very hard and sometimes almost impossible to see the opportunity which lies within the heart of every difficulty we face; but it is always there. The first step out of quiet, noisy, or any other sort of desperation is to take a fresh look at the meaning of your life. *You are here to reach for the stars, to realize your potential, to grow in self-awareness and to share your developing consciousness with others.* When you are doing this you will feel centred, purposeful and fully alive and nothing can hold you back. Your life will become positive and meaningful when you stop complaining about your 'problems' and see them instead as 'challenges' which you will overcome. This is an entirely new take on the way that most people view their lives: the old moaning, problematic style doesn't work and never will; let it go.

TASK 17 ....

Rising to the Challenge

You have taken this important first step, out of hopelessness and blame and into optimism and creativity, by buying and reading this book. So let's grasp the nettle and now move straight to a consideration of your lessons.

Bring to mind an ongoing problem, one that seems to keep popping up (your energy has probably already dropped at the mere thought of it). Write a brief, factual description of it in your journal. Now, decide to take a fresh look at this by keeping your energy upbeat and viewing your 'problem' as a 'challenge'. Notice how the different terms extract a different energetic response from you. The word 'problem' brings images of obstacles and limits (no wonder we feel tired at the very mention of the word). However, we can 'rise to' and overcome a challenge. So can you rise to this particular challenge of yours. The lesson will always ask you:

• to *recognize* that you keep attracting this challenge,
• to *understand* why you continue to do this,
• to *change* your energetic patterns so that you can move on.

Recognizing, understanding and changing is the process we use when we develop our self-awareness and overcome our personal obstacles. There is nothing standing in your way that you cannot step over!

....

Recognizing Your Patterns

'It is our attitude that allows us to view difficulties as lessons or opportunities, challenges instead of setbacks.'

JULIA CAMERON

When the next crisis appears on your horizon, take a deep breath and don't collapse in a heap of misery. You can rise to this challenge: look for the opportunity to increase your self-awareness and improve your life. Life is like a mirror; it reflects to you all the beliefs, mental pictures and behaviour that you are radiating. And so, instead of falling apart at the cruelty and unfairness of life, use the challenge as a doorway to a deeper understanding of yourself. Look into the mirror of your life for a true reflection of precisely where you are at.

Whenever your life presents you with a repeat showing of an event or situation, or even a feeling, take notice! In pursuit of self-awareness, repeats are vital clues. Of course, if the patterns are positive and creative they mirror your enthusiasm and upbeat energy: positive patterns reflect your optimism and self-confidence. However, negative patterns reflect your unhappiness and low self-esteem; they take you round and round in a negative spiral and they wear away your hope and trust. Does ——— *always* happen to you? Can you *never* do ———? Does your low self-belief *continually* let you down? Do you *keep* attracting poor relationships? Are you *constantly* concerned with your body image?

Are you *always* worried about money? These phrases are an indication of repeating negative patterns. Consider what your own life is reflecting to you. Think particularly about the areas of your life where you are feeling stuck and unable to move forward. Refer to the Assessment of Your Life Zones in your personal journal and look at your feelings, beliefs and hopes and fears surrounding these difficult areas. The great news is that, once you recognize and understand your negative patterns, you can let them go.

Understanding Yourself

Why do we hang on to negative patterns which only create limitations, unhappiness and discontent in our lives? Why do we keep attracting failure and lack of success and joy? We don't do this consciously, of course; in fact, we are so unconscious of how we do it that we usually manage to find someone else to blame for our 'bad luck'. The truth is that we sabotage ourselves by radiating negative thought, emotional and behaviour patterns. And at the root of these patterns lies a need to destroy our achievements, *because we believe that we don't deserve success.* If we hold critical beliefs about ourselves then we will never believe that we deserve the best and so we will never allow ourselves to have the best. This is such a crucial point and again highlights the importance of positive self-belief. If, in the deepest part of myself, I really don't think that I am 'good enough' and 'worthy enough' to be a winner, then I will always make sure that I lose. My unconscious is the genie of my lamp and for all the time I'm hanging on to my lack of self-worth my genie will ensure that I only ever get exactly as much as I think that I deserve. If you have a low sense of self-worth then it's costing you dear. If you want to turn your life around it's time to give your genie another message! *Know thyself* is the first counsel written over the gateway to the temple at Delphi. In knowing and appreciating yourself you learn everything you need to know to create happiness and fulfilment, this is the key to effective change.

Changing

No one has a clear path through life. When we encounter people who are really making a go of it we are inclined to think that they have been especially blessed or showered with lucky breaks. This isn't true of course; their motivation to achieve their potential, and their boundless energy in pursuit of this quest, come from a change of attitude. We can choose whether to make our journey a compassionate and enjoyable process of self-exploration or whether to embark on the painful path of self-criticism and doubt. Compassion or criticism, which road will you take? Self-knowledge leads to the uncovering of our critical patterns: there really is nothing to be gained from beating ourselves up with negative self-beliefs. We have all internalized so many critical beliefs about ourselves and we believe them to be true. Of your critical self-beliefs, 99.9 per cent are untrue! Why do you *ever* believe that you are less than amazing! Those messages from babyhood have slipped into your unconscious to create the programme that you are running on now! If you were invalidated as a small child you will believe that deep down you are no good and don't deserve to be supported.

Yesterday I saw a child in a pushchair at the supermarket and she was crying and moaning. Her mother (who was pushing a trolley as well as the pushchair) had come to her wits' end. I'm sure she loves her little girl dearly but eventually, when she picked her up out of her pushchair to give her a cuddle, she said, 'Oh, Laura, why are you always such a pain?' She didn't mean her daughter any harm, but of course this is not the harmless statement it seems. If as a child you are told that you are 'always such a pain' or 'always getting in the way' or 'always get things wrong', or that you are silly, stupid, too fat, not pretty, too thin, just hopeless etc. you will store these messages in your unconscious and these beliefs will underlie your patterns in adult life. Think about your own self-beliefs, what do you believe about yourself and why? How are these beliefs affecting your relationships, and your self-image? Do they create a glass ceiling in your work and money-making zones?

If you are struggling with self-doubt and criticisms you need to shine the light of consciousness on your negative self-beliefs. It is not always easy to know what these are but it is certainly possible. Bring your negative thoughts to light and replace them with positive affirmations and visualizations. It really is this easy! When the next energetic and motivated person enters your life, know that this is what they are doing; they have become conscious of their self-critical beliefs and they are changing them for positive affirmations that work. Living well is an art form, learn the techniques and create new realities for yourself. The only obstacle in your way is your lack of self-belief.

TASK 18

Your Positive Affirmations

Start to replace your self-criticisms by making positive and supportive affirmations about yourself. Choose some from the list below or compose your own (but be sure that you are making positive statements, in the present tense).

1   I am always good enough.
2   I am sensitive and clever.
3   I am a loving person.
4   I appreciate and value myself.
5   My contribution is always important.
6   I deserve the best in life.
7   I am a winner.
8   I am always doing my best.
9   I am highly motivated.
10   I am ready to change.

If you feel silly when you say these positive things about yourself that's quite a natural reaction (we are so used to just bringing ourselves down); just ignore these feelings. If you think you can't say them because they aren't true, ignore these thoughts as well. Keep what you are doing to yourself until you feel more confident (don't give other people's cynicism a chance to sabotage your efforts). You can write your affirmations on a piece of card and prop it up at your desk or over the sink or in your car. You can sing your affirmations to your favourite tune. Be creative, keep it light, have fun with this and watch for changes. A positive self-belief is always a bigger thought than a negative belief (remember the pebbles in the pond). The waves of your bigger thoughts will overpower your smaller negative ripples. Stick at this task for fabulous results!

....

The Devil We Know

Logically speaking, there is absolutely no reason on earth why we should continue to behave in ways that bring us misery. If you have ever observed a relationship where a man abuses a woman in some way (cheats on her, hits her, humiliates her, bullies her) you will certainly have wondered why she stays with him. Is it love of the man? No, it's love of his patterns. She stays because she is comfortable being victimized. Hard to believe? Impossible to accept? Yes; logically speaking, this analysis just doesn't hold together. The example of the abused woman returning for more of the same treatment has been well documented in psychological theory. There are reams of depressing statistics that show that even if women 'who love too much' (allow men to victimize them) get away from the abuser they most often just go on to find other victimizers to run their life.

Think of an electric light in your house. Normally, you switch it on or off as required, but were the switch to develop a short-circuit, the light would stay on all the time. Your energy is like a mass of electrical circuits controlled by an infinite number of switches. The circuits which have most influence on your life are those which have been hot-wired to bypass their switches. One day you might have a passing thought that you are being 'a bit of a pain', but this is not a hot-wired circuit which underlies your belief patterns and so the thought is simply switched off and has little or no effect on you. Now, if little Laura in the supermarket is *continually* blamed for 'always being such a pain', this is very likely to become a hot-wired message for her, one that cannot be switched off, and so will bring with it its attendant behaviour and emotional patterns. So you see how our underlying belief patterns short-circuit the main theme and create subplots and repeating scenarios which illuminate our lives. If I felt abused or abandoned as a child, one of my short-circuits would tell me that I was worthless and didn't deserve love. This feeling would be so familiar that it would become a comforting light for me. I would be drawn to repeating relationships which reflect my worthlessness and inability to obtain love. Logic and reason would become irrelevant; I would be irresistibly attracted to men who were bad for me, just as men with abusing patterns would be attracted to me – like a moth to a light bulb!

We can become obsessed by repeating our old hurts because:

- they are what we recognize and so at a very deep level we feel secure (the devil we know);

- if we keep repeating the pattern, we think there is always a chance that we might break it (by changing someone's behaviour and so mending the original hurt).

Yes, it's true, when we are deep in our patterning we are neither logical nor reasonable. When our switches are short-circuited we all become wholly emotional and irrational; men too!

Facing Our Fear of Change

When we replace negative, critical patterns with positive and expansive ones and support our new ways of thinking with creative visualization, we can become hot-wired for success. It sounds easy, indeed it is easy, so why aren't we all busy doing it? Well, as we have seen, old habits die hard and change can be frightening, even if it promises great things. We love the familiar and tend to cling to the known, in a search for safety and sameness in a world that moves so fast. It seems that we will even hang on to patterns that bring us grief in a search for the security we crave. The irony is that we can only find this safety, comfort and security within our own hearts; when have learned to appreciate and love ourselves and to know that we deserve the best.

And then of course there's that thorny issue of 'what people will think'. We might wonder why this should matter in any way when we are talking about such an important issue as changing our lives for the better. Who cares if your new assertive approach upsets the neighbours? What does it matter if your wonderful new relationship makes your friends envious? Your increased personal success will sort out your friends into two groups: those who are negative mirrors and those who are positive mirrors. Don't be afraid to let go of people who only reflect your negativity. Stick with those who support your new optimism and self-belief, these are your real friends. When you decide to change you will attract new people who match with your new vibrations. At the same time some people will leave your life because your energies will not attract each other any more. As soon as you start to stand up for yourself you will find that the victimizers from your old life will either change their behaviour towards you or they will leave. Embrace this chance to take control of your life; you have nothing to lose except your victim status. Let go of those who can't handle your success, welcome positive change and become a winner – decide to just do it now!

There are no obstacles to your success unless you believe that there are.

Key Points for Contemplation

1 You are not alone with your problems.

2 There is an art to living well; learn this art.

3 Your life is a training course in how to live.

4 Life's lessons come in the form of personal challenges.

5 If we don't learn from our lessons we have to repeat them until we do.

6 You are a work in progress.

7 The cyclical nature of life ensures that you will continually experience ups and downs.

8 There lies a hidden opportunity at the heart of every personal crisis; look for it.

9 You are here to reach for the stars, to realize your potential, to grow in self-awareness and to share your developing consciousness with others.

10 Your life will change completely when you stop complaining about your 'problems' and see them instead as 'challenges' which you will overcome.

11 Your lessons will always ask you to recognize, understand and change your patterns.

12 There is nothing standing in your way that you cannot step over!

13 Life is like a mirror and it reflects your patterns to you; look into the mirror of your life for a true reflection of where you are at.

14 We sabotage ourselves when we radiate negative thought, emotional and behaviour patterns.

15 If you have a low sense of self-worth you are paying for it with a low-quality life.

16 Learn to know and appreciate yourself; this is the key to positive, effective change.

17 No one has a clear path through life, we all have our individual lessons to learn.

18 Compassion or criticism, which road will you take?

19 Why do you ever believe that you are less than amazing?

20 How are your unconscious self-beliefs affecting your life zones?

21 Positive affirmations will replace your negative self-beliefs: a positive thought is always more powerful than a negative one.

22 We are drawn to repeating the patterns which we were used to in childhood; even abusive behaviour can feel secure and comfortable if it is familiar to us.

23 When our hot-wires are connected we all become wholly emotional and irrational.

24 Because we crave security and safety we are often afraid to change.

25 The comfort and protection we seek is only to be found within our own hearts; only when we can love and value ourselves will we feel secure.

26 Let go of the people who are your negative mirrors, whoever they may be.

27 Your true friends are your positive mirrors, you will know who these are.

28 There are no obstacles to your success unless you believe that there are!

Finding Harmony and Balance

'Happiness is not created as a result of certain conditions. Certain conditions are created as a result of happiness.'

The realities we create are a reflection of our own energetic processes. We don't create harmony and balance in our lives by looking for the conditions that create it. No, we look inside ourselves to find the balance and peace we seek *and then* it will become manifest in our lives. We change our outer circumstances by changing our inner awareness, because we attract whatever it is that we are radiating. We all know how true this is. Cast your mind back to a time when you were feeling out of sorts; you just weren't in the flow; you were certainly less than serene and your energy felt jagged. When you lose your calm centre and your energy feels scattered and unfocused, your world appears to be fragmented and disjointed; others feel very separate from you and it's difficult to remember that we are all connected. Everyone feels like this sometimes and some people feel like this most of the time.

The energy of the universe is naturally balanced and freely flowing unless it becomes blocked in some way by human interference. And, as we are part of this cosmic whole, our energy

96 | JUST DO IT NOW!

also flows freely unless this process becomes obstructed. When we are feeling good, centred and purposeful there is nothing we cannot achieve; we can realize our potential by integrating our energy in a harmonious and balanced way. Let's look at what this means in practice; how can we become balanced?

A Total Experience

You bring *all* of your energy to each of your experiences and, because you are a whole person, this energy comes from your mind, body, spirit and emotions. This holistic approach explains how we exist simultaneously at the spiritual, mental, emotional and physical levels and so bring all aspects of our humanness to each of our experiences. Figure 7 shows how this works.

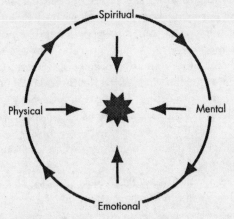

Figure 7 The Holistic Nature of an Experience

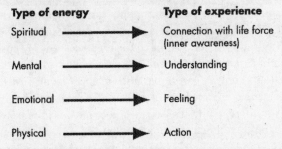

Type of energy	Type of experience
Spiritual	Connection with life force (inner awareness)
Mental	Understanding
Emotional	Feeling
Physical	Action

Figure 8 Levels and Experience

The next time you have an encounter with someone, become conscious of what is really going on; there are a number of levels of awareness interacting here. You each bring your own spiritual, mental, emotional and physical energies to this experience. Figure 8 shows how each 'type' of energy allows us a different 'type' of experience. You bring a spiritual experience of your own inner awareness, your own *connection* with the life force. You *understand* the encounter with your mental energy. Your emotional energy lets you have *feelings* about what is going on and your physical energy enables you to play an *active* part in this interaction. (For a more in depth discussion of the interplay of our energies please refer to my book, *Creating Self-Esteem*.)

When we bring together the 'types' of energy which we use at each level of our being we are able to have a whole and balanced experience. Of course our spiritual, mental, emotional and physical elements are not really separate: they are interactive, they affect each other and are mutually dependent. Our experiences are multidimensional. When the interplay of our energies is balanced, our *connecting, feeling, understanding* and *acting* come together to create a harmonious experience; we are going with the flow and life is sweet. But if we cannot smoothly integrate our energies then we feel less than our best and life becomes a struggle.

When I was a little girl my father was always giving me helpful tips and advice (and look where it led me!). One of the things he often used to say was, 'Work hard and play hard'. It has taken me many years to understand the meaning of this (being a person who always wanted to play rather than to work). I think that this aphorism demonstrates the meaning of balancing energy rather nicely: we need to spread our energy equally if we want to feel centred. Is your energy equally spread between your spiritual, mental, emotional and physical levels? Although our experiences of *connecting, understanding, feeling* and *acting* are interdependent, it's very useful to look at them separately to see where we might be blocking our energy. We are all unique and combine the four levels of energy in different ways. If we feel 'stuck', this means there is a block in the flow of energy in one or more of these levels. We only need to know where the flow is being obstructed and then we can act to clear the blockages.

What 'Type' of Person Are You?

Of course you experience your life with all of your energy. But until you have learned to balance your mind, body, spirit and emotions you will probably find that you often fall into one of the categories below.

Spiritual

Perhaps you are someone who can easily reflect on her 'inner life' and knows how to relax but can't bring this experience into material reality. In other words, you can *connect* but can't easily *act* upon this connection; you have an inspired imagination but can't put this into effect.

Mental

On the other hand, you might be a cerebral person, who is very good at *understanding* ideas and following concepts but finds it hard to act and be practical. Intellectual types also sometimes struggle to have experiences beyond those of the mind (difficulty in *connecting*).

Emotional

You might be the sort of person who is very sensitive to other people's *feelings*; you are emotionally aware and in touch with your own *feelings*, but does this gift sometimes cause you difficulties? Are you able to stop yourself from becoming so overwhelmed by your emotions that you are unable to *act?*

Physical

Or maybe you are good at *action* and can be counted upon to be practical in any situation, but you have little concept of anything beyond that which you can see in front of your eyes. If this is the case, you are having difficulties *connecting*.

You are so much more than the 'type' of person that you think you are! Open your heart and mind to your true potential. You are an amazing mortal, with the capacity to combine the grace of your spirituality, the magnificence of your mind, the heartfelt qualities of your emotions and the practical skills of your physical being. When this combination is balanced you feel centred, purposeful and in control of your own experiences. Balance is a key to creativity. Let's look at how we can set about re-balancing and optimizing our energies to bring creativity, harmony and meaning back into our lives.

Your Spiritual Energy – Connecting

'The source of love is deep within us …'

THICH NHAT HANH

When you activate your spiritual energy you are making a connection with the universal life force. We are often totally unaware of our spiritual nature, which can give us access to so much amazing inner knowledge and awareness. We live our daily lives as if 'what you see is what you get'; we live in this material world, acting as if that is all there is. Deep down we *know* there is more to life and we suffer profound dissatisfaction until we discover what is missing. When you have satisfied a material desire, how do you feel? Does that long-coveted designer dress bring lasting satisfaction? Can those new kitchen units bring you peace and contentment? Will that carton of ice-cream really improve your mood? Can you buy happiness? Peace, happiness, satisfaction, fulfilment and contentment are states of mind; they cannot be plucked from the material world because they can only be found inside you. The 'something more' which this materialistic society craves, exists within; it can only be found by our inner senses. Although we are called human beings and not human doings, we concentrate our activity in our doingness. Indeed, we often measure our success in terms of what we do and how much we are paid to do it. Our beingness relates to our spirituality and it is this quality which reminds us of our true calling. You were not created for the sole purpose of shopping, although this is what the modern media would have us believe. Perhaps this mania for the 'things' of the world is actually pushing us to seek our spiritual connection: who doesn't come back from the supermarket without thinking 'there surely must be something more to it than this'? And yes, of course there is more, and as soon as you start your search, clues begin to appear. Flashes of insight, a spark of intuition, synchronistic events, an opening of the heart, a deeper self-awareness, a new sense of meaning ... the link has been made.

This link is created by the divine spark of consciousness that we all share; it is the source of all life and without our spirit we would not be here. We are not human beings learning to be spiritual, we are spiritual beings learning to be human. And as we go through this process we sometimes forget our true purpose, which is *to realize our full potential as human beings*. If you are feeling jaded and disillusioned then your spiritual energy needs uplifting; your energy flow will be obstructed and you will feel out of balance.

Because the spiritual dimension of our lives can have such a profound effect on us, and considering our general neglect of this vital element, the next chapter, 'Loving Your Life', is all about spirituality. Meanwhile, you can begin to connect with your spiritual energy by learning to focus within. No, you don't have to trek to the Himalayas or spend hours contemplating the meaning of life, you only need to know *where* to look. It really is so simple but we often feel threatened by the thought of meditation and other 'spiritual' practices; they might seem strange and a bit 'other worldly'. Remember the wise counsel at Delphi, to *know thyself.* Learn to look within and you will indeed learn to know yourself.

Stopping Doing

Yes, you do need to withdraw from worldly activities to make your spiritual connection, but it's more about a subtle change in the focus of your awareness than a drastic change in your environment. You might find that the most difficult part of this task is actually allocating time for it. There is always so much to do, isn't there? How can we find the time for not doing and just being? A long time ago someone said to me, 'If you can't find time for yourself how can you expect anyone else to find time for you?' This stopped me in my ever-so-busy tracks and put me on a new road. Find the time, you are worth it! Take your personal journal and set out a weekly plan which shows when you will have time alone in order to do nothing and to be something. Even if you can only manage ten minutes a day this will be enough. Dedicate this time to being. Sit quietly and alone, turn off all electronic distractions and close your eyes in the silence. Expect nothing, just experience yourself. If you have never done this before it can be quite a shock: noises, feelings, thoughts (especially thoughts) are calling for your attention and ten minutes can feel like hours. Stick at this; learn to ignore your internal chatter (it never stops, so just let it go). This ten minutes a day is dedicated to being. Do this for a week and make a note of what happens and how you feel. In the next chapter we will move into more mind-expanding techniques.

....

Your Mental Energy – Understanding

'So much of what appears to be real in our lives is just a projection of a less-than-clear mind.'

BARBARA DE ANGELIS

Look back to your answers to Task 9, Your Self-Image (page 34). Review the lists where you scored 0 or 3. These self-beliefs create your self-image and radiate out into the world, where they create your realities. What sort of realities are your self-beliefs creating?

TASK 20 ....

Discovering Your Core Belief

Using your journal write down three adjectives which you think best describe you.

I am . . . .

I am . . . .

I am . . . .

Which of these statements is the most important? This is your underlying personal belief; your core self-belief. Does this statement validate you or criticize you?

....

Most of us are severely self-critical so the majority of you will be running with a negative core self-belief and this is a product of a less-than-clear mind. Whilst our unconscious mind is busy processing countless sensory messages, our conscious mind is constantly sorting reality to discover what we think is important and what we think is unimportant. This filtering process explains why we all perceive things differently; everyone's filter is different. Attention is energy and so we always get more of what we focus upon; negativity attracts more of the same. If your filter is based upon a critical core self-belief then life will always be difficult, and the only way you can change this is by creating a positively validating core self-belief. Let's examine why so many of us are using a negative filter.

Negative core beliefs have the following qualities:

- They are extremely critical.

- They often contain such words as 'useless', 'no good', 'worthless', 'too ...'.

- They are irrational and illogical.

- They perpetuate lack of confidence.

TASK 21 ....

Changing Your Mind

There is a wonderfully simple way to flush out our illogical, critical and demeaning self-beliefs so that we can hold them up to scrutiny and recognize that they are illusions. I first saw this technique described in Louise Hay's fabulous book *You Can Heal Your Life*, and I have used it successfully with countless people over the years. In order to pinpoint the source(s) of your limiting beliefs about yourself, you first make a 'should' list. Make a list of all the things that you think you 'should do', in your personal journal.

I should . . . .

I should . . . .

I should . . . .

I know that your list is long, because we are all manipulated by numerous 'shoulds', until we recognize that we are. Look at the following examples taken from the list of a client, John.

I *should* be fitter.
I *should* get more interested in DIY.
I *should* be more tolerant.
I *should* cut back on my drinking.
I *should* always be improving my education.
I *should* love my brother.
I *should* start getting up earlier.

I asked John to take each 'I should' and read it out loud and then to ask himself, 'Why should I?' Do this yourself with your own list. Make sure that you speak out loud, because when you give voice to your feelings it helps you to understand what is really going on. And what *is* going on? Put your answers in your journal. Some typical answers to the 'Why should I?' question are:

- Because people might not like me if I don't.
- My father/mother said I should.
- Because I'm too careless/thoughtless/lazy/untogether etc.
- Because everyone has to.

The answers to 'Why should I?' questions show us how we can limit ourselves by holding certain beliefs. The word 'should' always suggests that you were, are, or soon will become wrong in some way. Try ending one of your 'I should' statements with, 'because I really want to'.

Of course your sentence doesn't make sense because 'should' implies reluctance, guilt and fear. Do you really need to add to your burden of self-criticism and negativity in this way? Watch the words that you use (in thought as well as speech). Every time you think that you 'should', 'ought to' or 'must' do something, stop immediately and investigate the true meaning behind these thoughts.

By starting your should statements with, 'If I really wanted to' and replacing 'should' with 'could' you will get a whole new perspective on your perceived limitations. Let's take a look at what happens to John's list when it's revised in this way.

If I really wanted to I could be fitter.

If I really wanted to I could get more interested in DIY.

If I really wanted to I could be more tolerant.

If I really wanted to I could cut back on my drinking.

If I really wanted to I could always be improving my education.

If I really wanted to I could love my brother.

If I really wanted to I could start getting up earlier.

Can you see how different things look? John was utterly defeated by his 'should' list and yet his 'could' list offered insight and indicators for change. John immediately discovered two items that he had no desire to change: he had never been and would never be interested in DIY and he also felt no urge to be forever improving his education. These two items had preoccupied his parents: his father was always banging on about carpentry and home improvements whilst his mother was always trying to make her son more cultured. Look at your own revised list and weed out other people's preoccupations. Whose life are you living? John did want to get fitter and cut back on his drinking and somehow it now seemed possible to do something about these things. When you stop being a 'should' victim you become free to respond creatively and make appropriate changes. Getting up earlier, loving his brother and being more tolerant were also things that John felt that he could eventually work on but they came lower on his list of priorities. How does your list look? Isn't it fantastic to open those previously daunting critical doors and to welcome new creativity and energy into your life?

As soon as you let yourself off those critical hooks you will release new energy, creativity and motivation: just do it now!

....

Your Emotional Energy – Feeling

*'I wish thar was winders to my Sole, sed I,
so that you could see some of my feelins.'*

ARTEMUS WARD

We spend a lot of time, thought and money making our physical bodies as attractive as possible; take a look on your bathroom shelves, in your washbag, make-up bag, on your dresser, and you will see what I mean. We cut and tweezer, crimp and straighten, shampoo and condition, tone and moisturize; we wrap ourselves in seaweed and cake our bodies in mud, submit to electrolysis or waxing or even worse! It seems there are no lengths to which we won't go in pandering to the needs of the body we see in the mirror. But what of our emotional body, the one that can really wreak havoc with our lives if we don't care for it properly?

Do you cry at weepy films; get upset when you watch the news; feel unhappy when your loved ones are down; bounce about when you are happy? All these states are natural, our emotions are a part of us in the same way that our physical bits and pieces are. You might wonder how you can care for your emotional body when it seems to have such a life of its own. Feelings come and go, they can change in an instant: one minute you are feeling great and the next minute it's the pits. How can we live happily with our emotions when they can be so unpredictable?

We are often afraid of our feelings

Most of us have learned to 'protect' ourselves by not showing our feelings, the logic being that, if we show how we feel, we will become vulnerable to others and then somehow lose control. But this logic is illogical! It is a fear-based approach and as such is self-limiting and self-defeating as we become victims of our own emotions. Our feelings are directly related to our needs: when our needs are met we feel good and when they are not met we feel bad. If we deny our feelings we deny our needs and in so doing we devalue ourselves. So what if you are feeling depressed, ashamed, unhappy, chaotic, scared, embarrassed or sad? Everyone has to live with their emotions and we have the choice either to be tyrannized by them and live in fear or to enjoy them in a creative way. Our feelings show us our needs, and so they reflect the places where we need to work on our self-development and increased awareness.

Feeling, accepting and letting go

You might find it easier to show some feelings than others. As children we learn which emotions are 'acceptable' and which are 'unacceptable', and so certain feelings might have become taboo in some way. Picture a tiny child who showed her loving feelings and was then rejected; can you imagine how hard it would be for that grown-up child to demonstrate her love in her adult relationships? We are often taught to be afraid of our anger and so we 'bottle it up'. We all know what then eventually happens (usually at the most inappropriate time). Anger is a natural feeling and it is always a result of our own feelings of disempowerment. Often when we start to become more assertive and in control of our lives some of this old stored anger will emerge. Don't be afraid to feel angry: accept the feeling; look at your needs and see where they aren't being met; change your behaviour to support your needs (you might need to express your feelings to someone) and then let go. Why wish for 'winders to your Sole' when you can quite easily say what you are feeling? How can others know what you need if you can't show your emotions? If you keep pretending that you don't care for someone they will eventually believe you. If you pretend that you don't mind being treated like a doormat everyone will believe that too. If you act as if you are unemotional, people will treat you as if you have no feelings. Don't be afraid that your emotions will cause you pain; it is only denial which makes you hurt. *Feel free to feel*.

TASK 22

Coming out of Denial

Look at the following list of emotions and consider your relationship with each one. Ask yourself if you find it easy or hard (or somewhere in between) to accept and express each of these feelings.

Love	Happiness	Anger	Positivity	Depression
Delight	Hurt	Shame	Joy	Misery
Jealousy	Rejection	Grief	Harmony	Tenderness

Use your journal to make notes. Are there any interesting patterns emerging? Can you connect your attitude to certain emotions with anything that you remember from childhood? Are there any other emotions that affect you powerfully? Why do they? Is it difficult to relate to this exercise because you are finding it hard to get in touch with your true feelings? Whatever your answers, you are doing well. There are no ticks or crosses or marks out of ten. Remember that your life is a process of unfolding awareness and you are becoming more and more aware as you work your way through this book.

....

Your Physical Energy – Action

*'We teach people the ways
we want them to treat us.'*

LYNDA FIELD

I must have written this statement (or some version of it), in every one of my books. Its meaning lies at the very heart of the notion that we create our own reality: if we behave like a victim then we will be treated like one; if we respect ourselves then others will respect us. How are other people treating you? How do you act out there in the world? And, furthermore, are you acting or are you merely reacting? What messages are you communicating to others?

The ways that we think and feel find expression in our actions. By changing our negative beliefs, deepening our spiritual connection and learning to disclose our feelings we will eventually change the way that we behave. But we don't need to wait for deep personal changes to filter into our consciousness before we can alter our behaviour; we can learn a number of communication techniques which will hasten our development. Victims believe that they are born to be treated badly and that assertive people have had more chances in life. We have all experienced being victimized in some way, by our children, friends, colleagues, shop assistants (especially in clothes shops!), phone salespeople, waiters ... on a bad day the whole world can sometimes seem out to get us. We have seen that victim status is all about attitude; victim consciousness attracts loss, failure and more negativity whilst creative consciousness accepts personal responsibility, is assertive and attracts positivity and success.

Learning to Be Assertive

'Until one is committed, there is hesitancy, the chance to draw back, always ineffectiveness.'

GOETHE

Whenever we start blaming someone or something for whatever is going on that we don't like, we are copping out of our personal responsibilities; we are making an escape hatch so that we don't have to risk anything. The perceived risk is imaginary and it is always about fear of change. Forget these limiting mind games that produce illusory obstacles to your personal growth and increased awareness. *Just commit!* Commit to your own life. Decide to be the person you most want to be, no more hesitancy, no more escape hatches that only lead into ineffective behaviour. Committed and focused decisions attract the exact circumstances, people and events which are needed to activate them: *decisions are powerful magnets*. A strong desire to change provides the energy needed to create new and improved realities. We will activate this process in Section 3 of the book, when we look at possible action planning procedures in all of the life zones. Meanwhile, practise making decisions throughout your day. When you feel muddled and don't know what to think, just ask yourself this simple question: *What do I want to happen?* Then make a decision based on your answer. Don't spend hours chasing probabilities around in your head (that's exactly the sort of behaviour that created your indecision and muddle in the first place).

Once the decision is made it's time to act. What do you think is the difference between those who are (or who act as) losers and those who are winners? It has nothing to do with luck and everything to do with attitude and approach. It's not what you do that counts but rather how you do it. Winners and losers communicate differently and this is their defining feature. Go out and listen for victims. Notice the tone of voice as well as the actual words used – can you hear that 'poor me' whine? Now listen for non-victims – what differences can you hear? You can learn the techniques it takes to become assertive; anyone can become skilled at communicating if they are prepared to practise.

TASK 23 ....

6 Ways Towards Becoming Assertive

We will look at these techniques in greater detail in the last section of the book but for now just try to become aware of how assertive or non-assertive you are in different situations. Look at the list below and begin to try out some of these approaches.

1 *Be prepared to take risks* (no need to take up a dangerous sport, just be ready to make changes).
2 *Try to be less judgemental.* Withhold criticism and look for positive things to praise; people really respond to this approach.
3 *Become a listener.* You will be amazed by the effect this has. Refrain from having your say and listen actively. Everyone responds well to this treatment.
4 *Say what you mean* and mean what you say. Open and honest communication makes it easy for others to know where they stand with you.
5 *Be ready to say 'no'* when you have to. This little word is often hard to say. Practise! I promise you it gets easier and easier the more you say it. Remember, you can be a good friend and still say 'no'.
6 *Accept criticism calmly.* Maybe she's got a point? If not, then say what you feel, but rationally and not in the heat of anger (this carries much more authority).

These techniques help to open the lines of communication and will work to heal rifts and differences. The assertive communicator always comes from a place of respect and this helps others to respond appropriately.

Bringing It All Together

When your life feels good and you are motivated and enthusiastic you know that your energies are flowing freely (you are in the flow). And whenever this harmony is missing you know that your energy is blocked somewhere in the circuit. Although our spiritual, mental, emotional and physical energies are interdependent, it is often really useful to look at the four 'types' of energy separately, to find out exactly where the problem lies. Are you in touch with your spirituality; are you doing too much and being too little? What about your mental energy; are you operating from a series of 'musts', 'oughts' and 'shoulds'? Are you looking through a negative filter? Are you taking care of your emotional body? Can you accept and express your feelings or are you in denial over something? And how are you behaving out there in the world? Are you being assertive and taking responsibility for your actions or are you playing the victim? Run through this quick checklist when your energy is stuck and life isn't flowing easily through you. The natural world operates with checks and balances and we are a part of this cosmic flow. Check your energy and clear any blockages and maintain harmony and balance in your corner of the world.

Key Points for Contemplation

1 You exist simultaneously at the spiritual, mental, emotional and physical levels.

2 Peace, happiness and contentment are states of mind; they can only be found inside you.

3 There is a reason why we are called human beings and not human doings.

4 As soon as you start your spiritual search clues begin to appear: flashes of insight, a spark of intuition, synchronistic events, an opening of the heart ... the link has been made.

5 We are not human beings learning to be spiritual but spiritual beings learning to be human.

6 We sometimes forget our true purpose which is *to realize our full potential as human beings*.

7 Look within and you will learn to know yourself.

8 If you can't find time for yourself, how can you expect others to find time for you?

9 Much of what seems to be real in our lives is only a projection of a muddled mind.

10 Your self-beliefs create your self-image and radiate out into the world, where they create your realities.

11 Attention is energy and so we always get more of what we focus upon; watch your focus!

12 Are you still using a negative filter?

13 You can stop being a 'should' victim.

14 Let yourself off those critical hooks and release new energy and creativity.

15 Our feelings show us our needs and so they are a wonderful pointer to the places where we need to increase our awareness.

16 Anger is a natural feeling and it is always the result of our own feelings of disempowerment.

17 How can others know what you need if you don't show your true feelings?

18 Feel free to feel.

19 We teach people the ways we want them to treat us.

20 Just commit to your life; all else will follow.

21 Winners and losers communicate differently; communicate like a winner.

22 Be prepared to take risks.

23 Check your energy and keep clearing the emotional debris and you will maintain harmony and balance in your corner of the world.

9

Loving Your Life

'There are only two motives, two procedures,

Two frameworks, two results: Love and fear.'

LEUNIG

Positive and negative, abundance and scarcity, expansion and limitation, compassion and anger, hope and despair, tolerance and intolerance, appreciation and contempt, forgiveness and blame, creativity and victim behaviour ... two ways of looking at the world; two realities: love and fear.

Spiritual Literacy

Many people find it relatively easy to discuss and reflect upon their beliefs and behaviour but find it much harder to talk about their emotions and virtually impossible to consider their spiritual awareness. Most of us haven't had much practice at sharing our feelings and, in fact, have been actively discouraged from doing so. This lack of practice has given rise to a phenomenon which is called emotional illiteracy, whereby we are limited by a lack of useful vocabulary. We can't acknowledge our feelings because we just haven't got the words to describe them. Happily, this situation is improving as people are becoming more self-aware. Counselling has become mainstream and there is a growing understanding that it is good to talk about our feelings. But as we are developing our emotional literacy it is becoming increasingly obvious that we are struggling to find the words to express our spirituality. There is still a lot of confusion surrounding this word 'spiritual' and people are very anxious to know exactly what is meant by it. Does it have anything to do with religion, and if so which religion? Do I have to believe in God? Does it have anything to do with dead people, cults of any sort, voodoo, frightening and unusual behaviour? Is it unworldly and does it lead to madness? Will I have to change my behaviour and stop doing all the things I like doing? Will I have to wear strange clothes and eat lentils or spend hours in meditation? Will I see ghosts and levitate and speak with the dead? Will I have to stop playing football, drinking wine, dyeing my hair, going to the pub? (Add any of your own fears to this list.)

All Human Beings Are Spiritual Beings

Because we are human, we are naturally spiritual. Universal energy flows through us and we are all connected to that divine spark of consciousness which gives us life. *Our spirituality gives us our love of life.* Rather than looking for external examples of what it is to be spiritual we need only look inside to feel the in*spir*ation and joy that our spiritual nature brings. Sounds suspiciously easy? Surely it can't be that simple? But yes, it is. Anyone who has ever seen a newborn baby will know that they arrive encased in glorious energy; they emanate their spirituality and you can *feel* the divine spark within them. And so you came, trailing your clouds of glory, and then you started to get busy learning how to become an earthling. Very soon your material preoccupations filled your life and you were so absorbed in 'doing' that you lost touch with your 'being'. Connecting with your spirituality is not a new procedure for you. This is not a journey into a strange and unknown world, but a reconnection with an experience that you have known all along but have forgotten about.

Just Doing Nothing

> *'Spiritual growth is the single most important thing you can focus on if you want a joyful, peaceful and loving life.'*

SANAYA ROMAN

You can't *Just Do It* effectively unless you know how to *just do nothing*. Our being and doing must be balanced in order for us to create lives that are positive, loving, compassionate, joyful and appreciative. In the previous chapter, when we looked at the importance of balancing our spiritual, mental, emotional and physical energies we touched on the true nature of our life's purpose. We are here on earth *to realize our full potential as human beings*, and to do this we must connect with our spirituality. When we open up to our spiritual dimension we open our lives to new meaning and purpose.

So let's begin by just doing nothing in order that we can hear our own spiritual voice. A strong intention always brings results, so as soon as you are ready to embrace your spirituality, amazing things will begin to happen. Twenty years ago, when I began my spiritual pursuit in earnest (I *really* wanted to know what it was all about), the universe showered me with gifts. I met a wonderful spiritual teacher, was led to the perfect books, experienced incredible synchronistic events and felt that suddenly I understood that my life had a meaning and purpose which I hadn't recognized before. One of the most important things that happened to me at this time was that I began to hear, listen to, and act upon the voice of my intuition.

Guided by Intuition

How many times have you had a strong desire to do something and then dismissed it because it didn't seem rational, only to find out later that it would have been just the right action to take?

What about that time when you just knew about something which was happening miles away from you? And then, of course, there are those constant inner nudges which tell you that your judgement is at fault or that your hunch is right. Our spirit speaks to us in many ways and one of its voices is our intuition. Our super-rational culture encourages us to reason things out rather than to act on our instincts and so we are often disinclined to look for answers which are other than reasonable. But there is a wise and intuitive part of you where you can always turn for sound answers and true understanding; the keys to awareness are within you. Trust your intuitive voice.

TASK 24 ....

Listening to Your Intuition

Can you remember a time when you acted upon your intuition and things turned out well? What about a time when you 'knew' that you should do something but you didn't follow your gut feeling and things went badly for you? Now think about your life at the moment. What intuitive guidance have you received recently? This might involve small changes: get the car serviced; phone a friend; take some time out for yourself; read that book. Or it may be pointing to much larger issues: end that relationship; stop smoking; train for a new job. Make a note of your answers in your journal. Have you acted on this guidance? If not, why not? Sometimes we just don't want to do what our heart and soul are telling us to do. When we receive inner guidance to make major changes in our lives we would often rather not listen and just keep on with our usual routine. If your intuition is sending strong messages that you are disregarding, then dissatisfaction and unhappiness are close at hand.

Start to make a habit of listening to your inner voice. Whenever you are uncertain of a decision or unsure how to act, take a moment to hear what your intuition is telling you. This might seem quite difficult at first, but the more you are prepared to listen the clearer the messages will become. Meanwhile, act on hunches, gut feelings, flashes of insight and feelings of 'knowingness' and see where they take you. Trust your inner knowing and it will guide you towards amazing new experiences. Your intuitive guidance is always leading you to realize your full potential and so to make your life a positive and creative experience.

....

Looking at the Bigger Picture

When things aren't going so well it's easy to lose trust in our-selves and the universe. How did I get into this mess? Why can't I get a grip on my life? Why is everything going wrong? There are only two realities, love and fear, and when we lose trust we go into a fearful, negative or victim state. When our energy is stuck and we are in victim mode it is very hard to see the meaning and purpose behind what is unfolding: we are struggling with imme-diate problems and have no time, energy or inclination to look at the bigger picture of our lives.

Picture yourself in a boat, travelling along a winding river where you can only see the water a few metres behind you and ahead of you. Now think of this river as the river of your life and imagine it from an aerial view. Looking down you can see all the twists and turns and which tributaries lead to where. When you connect with your spirituality you transcend that which imme-diately surrounds you; you see more than that which is in front of your eyes. The bigger picture of your life shows you *why* things are happening to you, why you have been led in a certain direc-tion and how these situations and experiences have been absolutely necessary for you to complete a future stage of your life.

TASK 25 ....

Drawing Your Lifeline

Take a large sheet of paper and draw your lifeline. Start at birth and draw a line which represents the important ups and downs in your life. This line doesn't have to be to scale or be a work of art (unless you want it to be), but do make a note of significant points. I have used this technique many times in workshops and people always experience new personal insights and revelations as they look at the bigger picture of the events in their lives. If I hadn't met her then I never would have ... *I took that decision then never realizing how it would affect me all these years later ... Who would have guessed how that period of depression would have led me to a turning point in my career ... When that terrible relationship ended I was distraught, but now I look back and think it was the best thing that could have happened to me ...* Look for the connections and meaningful coincidences in your own lifeline. Look for the threads of guidance that have led you from one seemingly unconnected event to another. Search for the link between cause and effect and see the synchronicity at work in your life. You are always being guided by the voice of your spirit. When you connect with the divine spark of universal energy you will receive insights and revelations which will help you to see the 'why' behind the 'what' (oh, so that's why that happened, I can see the reason behind it now).

Love and Fear

> *'Love is all you need.'*
>
> LENNON AND MCCARTNEY

There really are only two frameworks within which we can create our realities. Do you remember in the Introduction when we looked at the positive/negative line between numbers 5 and 6 of the Scale of Feelings? Look back to page 2 now and you will see that we cannot feel slightly negative or a bit positive, we can only be one or the other. Any answer below 6 in your Life Zone Checklist places you in negative mode and 6 and above puts you in the positive cycle; *there is no place in between*. The negative cycle is grounded in fear and its key features are: limitation and scarcity (there will never be enough to go around); anger, intolerance and victim behaviour (people are better/worse than me); blame, despair and contempt (poor me/how come my life isn't working?/it's all *their* fault). The positive cycle is grounded in love – love of self, the universe and all that dwells in it. A loving consciousness develops from our innate spirituality: *our spiritual connection gives us our love of life.* If we cannot connect with the divine nature within us, we will never be able to love our lives, and so will stay stuck in the fearful, negative cycle. So, it becomes clear that we can only lift ourselves into a positive cycle if we embrace the love we find in our hearts and souls. Yes, it's true, all you need is love!

Let's look at the principal characteristics of the positive cycle. Love is the key and reveals itself in belief, trust and faith in self and the process of life. Self-belief demonstrates itself in enthusiastic and motivated behaviour (yes, I can rise to this challenge and I will). It's interesting to note that the word 'enthusiasm' stems from the Greek words *en-theos*, which means 'to be in God', and in a very real sense we can see how our spirituality (or lack of it) helps to create our own realities. When we are choosing the framework of love and positivity we embrace an expansive awareness; our hearts and minds are open and we are able to feel compassion for ourselves and others. If, like Dr Seuss' Grinch, your heart feels 'two sizes too small', you can always help it to grow.

TASK 26 ....

Opening Your Heart

Did you know that your heart will open if you:

Find something to appreciate. Put on your appreciative eyes and go out and look for something to appreciate. Keep looking until you feel your heartstrings tug. Some things you could look for are: small flowers growing in the cracks in the pavement, a bird singing just for the joy of it, a smile from a stranger, any act of kindness ... leave your judgements behind and look for beauty and you will find it.

Tell someone how much you they mean to you. Write a letter, send an email, phone a friend, give someone a hug ... give your love, with no strings attached and you will feel great.

Look into a mirror and say to yourself, 'I am good enough, just the way I am.' This might make you cry (remember, this is also a sign that your heart has been moved).

Create something. A cake, a meal, a tidy room. Put a bunch of flowers on the table, light a candle. Give the project (however small) all of your attention. Admire the results: you can and do make a difference. Someone once said that we are here to learn how to live and not how to win. Feel glad, just to be alive.

Jump for joy, even if you have to pretend to feel joyful. Fake it until you make it. Jump as high as you can and shout 'I love my life'. An emotional reaction is guaranteed (both laughter and tears are demonstrations of heart feelings).

Smile at a stranger and watch for their reaction. If you chose someone who didn't know how to smile back then try someone else.

Forgive someone. This one deserves a paragraph all of its own!

....

Forgiving Ourselves and Others

For me, forgiveness is the most important issue in self-development; it moves negative energy faster than any other technique and it brings with it the great spiritual gifts of calm, peace, balance and compassion. Before you react too strongly to this (why should I forgive him/her after what he/she did to me?) stop and reconsider which framework creates positive realities and which one creates negative realities. We know that anger, intolerance, and blame are grounded in fear and keep us stuck in limiting behaviour patterns. A life based upon love brings all the enthusiasm, joy and inspiration that we could wish for ourselves; and love starts here, with ourselves. Many people find the concept of self-love very hard to handle (isn't this egotistical/selfish/narcissistic?). Everything is connected, we are all part of the divine web of creation, we are spiritual beings and we need to respect our origins. Each time we treat ourselves badly we are disrespecting the miracle of life; every time we limit ourselves we deny the highest potential that human beings can achieve; whenever we fail to find love in our hearts for ourselves we will fail to love others. Forgive yourself for all your perceived 'failings'; you are so much more than a bundle of mistakes. Forgiveness means letting go. So, let go of all the things you 'should' have done. Let go of all the times that you have been mean and hurtful. Guilt keeps you locked into negativity and will never, ever inspire you to become the person you most want to be. If you have made mistakes (as we all have), learn from them, apologize if necessary and then move into a more productive cycle. *You cannot love and appreciate others if you do not love and appreciate yourself.* How would you be able to recognize the greatness in other human souls if you had not first felt it in your own heart?

And so to forgiving others. Any old hurts, angers and hatreds that you carry for others just sit in your energy field attracting more of the same. Thoughts are magnets and as we send out negative energy we create a pathway for it to return to us; a fantastic reason to get to grips with forgiveness. Remember that *forgiveness means letting go,* it does *not* mean that you don't care if people treat you badly. It's so amazing that we can spend more time thinking about the people who have hurt and upset us than we do about those who care for us and support us. Step out of this harmful trap; you will never be able to love and appreciate yourself whilst you are carrying poisonous thoughts about others. Forgiveness of others calls for a radical rethink of your past hurts: lift out of victim consciousness into creative consciousness; ask yourself, 'What can I learn from what happened?'

TASK 27 ....

4 Steps to Forgiveness

1 *State the facts* View whatever happened as objectively as possible. At first you might have to pretend that it happened to someone else in order to get a true perspective. Write down the facts in your journal. Stick to the reality and don't embroider it

with your emotions. So, for example, you might have written, *my mother was an alcoholic when I was growing up.*

2 *Accept the facts* Don't get lost in blame and tears, you are no longer a victim of the past. A creative response (non-blaming) will allow you to move forward and leave the hurt behind, so be creative in your approach. If you need to express your feelings about what happened then make sure you do so but don't get stuck in repeated emotional discharge (this might feel like you are working through something when you are really only going over and over the same issue).

3 *Decide to let go* This is a defining moment. Are you ready to let go or are you still gaining more from moaning, blaming and complaining? Once you have definitely confirmed your desire to forgive, then the process really starts moving. Don't expect 100 per cent success immediately, it might take a while. Sometimes it's only possible to forgive a bit at a time (I can forgive *this* but not *that* at the moment). Later you might bring yourself to let go of *that*, but only if you can hang on to something else. Forgiveness is a process which has a thinning effect on the wounds of the past and eventually they are thinned out of existence.

4 *Enjoy the freedom* that your forgiveness brings. The more you can forgive, the lighter you will feel, as you free up your energy for more positive use.

....

Deepening Your Spiritual Connection

Creative visualization is a powerful technique which will enhance your spiritual development. Remember when we talked about getting into a 'relaxed state' in the chapter on creative visualization? Well, go to page 63 (Task 14) and remind yourself of the procedure. In this relaxed state I want you to create a sanctuary for yourself; a place where you are comfortable and feel at home. This could be a paradise isle or a mountain chalet, a place of great natural beauty or a cosy room filled with the things you love. In other words, create the retreat of your dreams. Give yourself some time to create the details (a comfortable chair, a garden of wild flowers, an ocean view, the perfume of pine needles ...). Allow yourself to become totally familiar with your beautiful new environment. This is your sanctuary and you can retreat here at any time. Very soon you will just be able to close your eyes and be here in an instant. Your sanctuary is a spiritual retreat where your heart can open to new and wondrous realities. Know that when you bring your problems here they will be unravelled and healed. Here you can speak with your intuition, releasing your hopes and fears and asking for guidance. This is also a marvellous place to bring your forgiveness issues. In the comfort and security of your sanctuary you can visualize those people with whom you have unfinished business, and then finish it. When you visualize a conversation between you and another person it has real meaning and consequences. Your thought magnets and your strong intention to forgive and let go will have a profound effect in the real world. Try this and see. Create forgiveness in your sanctuary and then feel the benefit in your life. Each time you use your sanctuary for positive change and healing it becomes imbued with greater spiritual power and grace.

Coming from Your Deepest Truth

Two ways of looking at the world, two realities: love and fear. When you are positive, upbeat, hopeful, appreciative, forgiving and open hearted you are coming from your deepest truth; you are coming from love. This is a place where you are able to express your feelings and feel self-respect and self-worth. When you are being true to yourself you stand by your own values and live their reality. If you find yourself being manipulated by others or being made to feel wrong in some way, you are able to be true to your own feelings and to be assertive. Whenever you are feeling victimized this is a sign that you have not stood by your own beliefs and have allowed someone to take away your power. Your deep spiritual connection reminds you that you are first and foremost a *spiritual* being who is learning to be human.

Never forget that you are rooted in spirit and in love and that you have your own perfect place in this world. Live your truth; stand by your ideals; treat others with respect; love and appreciate yourself and the realities you create will be wondrous and joyful.

Key Points for Contemplation

1 There are only two frameworks, two realities: love and fear.

2 Because we are human we are naturally spiritual.

3 Our spirituality gives us our love of life.

4 Connecting with your spirituality does not involve a journey into a strange and unknown world, but a reconnection with an experience that you have known all along.

5 When we open to our spiritual dimension we open our lives to new meaning and purpose.

6 As soon as you are ready to embrace your spirituality, amazing things will begin to happen.

7 The keys to awareness are within you; trust your intuitive voice.

8 Sometimes we just don't want to do what our heart and soul are telling us to do.

9 Your intuitive guidance is always leading you to realize your full potential.

10 The bigger picture of your life shows you why things are happening to you.

11 Look for the threads of guidance that have led you from one seemingly unconnected event to another.

12 Love is all you need.

13 Keep your heart and mind open.

14 You cannot love and appreciate others if you do not love and appreciate yourself.

15 Forgive yourself and set yourself free.

16 Forgive others and your life will change completely.

17 Go to your sanctuary to deepen your spiritual connection.

18 Live your truth, respect yourself at all times; trust the process of life and remember that you are a spiritual being.

19 Two realities, love and fear: choose love every time!

Some Frequently Asked Questions About the Spiritual Dimension

As the general interest in spiritual matters grows and develops, I have noticed that many more people are asking for clarification about the nature of our spirituality. I am including here a short list covering some of the frequently asked questions on the subject. You might find that some of these queries and concerns are issues for you too.

Q *I don't like the term 'spiritual'; it just makes me cringe, it has religious overtones for me and I am an atheist. How can a non-believer be in touch with his spirituality? I am confused about this.*

A It is easy to be confused by all the different ways that spirituality has been defined. Some people believe in God and that is their definition; others have a sense of a natural order and pattern which gives their lives meaning; some link with an awareness of the divine spark within all living things; others feel a connection with a greater part of themselves which they call their higher self. There are as many ways to define spirituality as there are people on the planet and here lies the important truth: your sense of the spiritual is personal, unique and yours alone. Don't worry about what the words mean; they mean different things to different people. Remember that the spiritual dimension takes you *beyond* words and beyond a logical definition. Learn to *feel* your spiritual connection and when you do the experience will bring answers to your questions.

Q *I'm really thrilled with the results I'm getting from using affirmations and creative visualization techniques. At last I'm finding the strength to tackle my problems. The trouble is, my family won't take me seriously. They hate seeing my affirmations stuck up on the wall and they laugh at me when I meditate. I keep telling them how amazing it all is but they won't listen to me. I know how much good it would do my husband if he started to meditate. My husband says I'm turning into a hippy with all my New Age ideas and all this domestic aggro is causing lots of new problems for me.*

A I'm very glad that you raised this issue because it is such a common concern. When we first make a meaningful spiritual connection it's so exciting and mind expanding that we want to tell the world all about it. Unfortunately, the rest of the world (and in particular your family members) will not show the slightest interest and probably will take exception to what you have to share with them. There are two things to consider here. First, you cannot change anyone else, however much you want to! Your nearest and dearest are probably feeling threatened by your evangelicism and the affirmations on the wall are just rubbing salt into the wounds. Second, your spiritual development can be likened to a sapling, which needs to be protected and nurtured until it is strong enough to stand alone. In other words, keep your new activities to yourself. Keep meditating; take down your affirmations and keep them in cards in your pocket. As you grow spiritually you will see the effects in all areas of your life and your family will see the changes, too. The very best way to advertise the benefits of spiritual practice is to live the results. When your family members see the new calm and happy you they might even start to wonder what these 'New Age' ideas are all about.

Q *I keep hearing people talking about 'listening to the voice of your intuition'. I have no idea what this means. How do I know when my intuition is speaking to me?*

A Yes, it is tricky to hear that voice to begin with, but it gets easier the more you practise. It's unlikely that you will actually hear a voice; you are more likely to have a gut feeling about something or a strong sense of knowingness. A good way to develop contact with your intuition is to take 'checking-in breaks' during the day. Every now and then, whatever you are doing, just stop and check in with your intuition. What are you feeling? How are things going? Do you feel moved to act in a certain way? If you have an intuitive flash quickly followed by a doubting voice (oh no, I couldn't possibly do that), just notice if this flash comes back to you. When your intuition repeats itself it's sending an important message; take notice and act! Have an Intuition Week. Make notes throughout the week on the consequences of following and not following your intuition. One important clue to recognizing the message of your intuition: when you follow it you will feel great because your energy is flowing where it is meant to flow.

Q *You say that forgiveness opens the heart and releases nega0tivity and I suppose this is right. But there is someone in my life who I absolutely detest, she took away my husband and they share custody of my children with me. It feels like I spend my whole life thinking about her and wishing she was dead, I am not free to get on with my own life. Please advise me.*

A I am so sorry that you find yourself in this dilemma, it sounds very painful. I think you know that you cannot carry on like this without consuming yourself with hatred and affecting your children in a harmful way. Let's go back to the facts. Your husband has left you for another woman; presumably he decided to leave (even though it feels like she took him away from you). They have set up home together and you are in constant communication over the children. Your hatred for this woman is ruining your life. Why are you prepared to wreck your life for her? Do you want a life of your own? If so, you must act quickly. So you can't forgive her – well, why not just accept the facts of the situation? Decide to let go of her influence on you and each time your mind turns to hash over the same old blaming stuff, just STOP. Keep putting a stop on this habit and slowly but surely you will gain a larger perspective. The next steps will follow easily. I know it's hard to believe that there is a life for you beyond your anger towards this woman, but of course there is. Let go in small bites and before you know it she will be out of your mind.

Q *I want to be a spiritual person and love everybody all the time but sometimes I get very angry. How can I become more spiritual, calmer and learn to keep my temper?*

A What a wonderful question this is. Oh to be a 'spiritual' person: calm, centred, loving and kind, a saint in fact! You *are* a spiritual person (your spirituality lies within) but you are probably not in the line for a sainthood and nor are many of us. You cannot love everyone all of the time and if you did your judgement would be seriously questionable. And you get angry? Another totally natural reaction. Spiritual people are ordinary folk, living ordinary lives; they lose their tempers and are less than perfect *but they keep on working on themselves.* Let yourself off the hook, be yourself and keep up with the spiritual practices. As your spirituality develops you will find it easier to moderate your moods and limit the effect that others have on your emotions. Keep up the good work.

Living Dynamically

10

Begin It Now!

'Whatever you can do or dream you can, begin it.
Boldness has genius, power and magic in it.
Begin it now.'

GOETHE

In this final section of the book you will apply the principles of creativity to changing your own realities in the different life zones. Look back again to the Life Zone Checklist on page 2. You can expect to improve all your original scores and certainly you can take yourself above the positive/negative line in all aspects of your life, if you really want to! The following chapters will look in detail at your self-image, relationships, health and fitness, money issues and work. You know the techniques and we will look at how to apply them, so that you will be able to create a personal action plan for change in each of your life zones.

Over the years I have worked with many people who have successfully changed and improved their lives. It takes effort, commitment and a strong desire to move ourselves out of our old habitual patterning into something new and fresh and positive. You notice that I said that you can move into the positive cycle, *if you really want to*. Well, you might wonder who would possibly choose to stay in the negative mode and deny themselves the chance of a fulfilled and happy life, with supportive relationships, a good income and a satisfying career. That person might be you! There are a number of reasons why, even at this stage, you might decide not to change.

Choosing Not to Change

Let's face the facts, the old comfortable behaviour patterns are just like a worn out pair of slippers: the soles might be dropping off but they are just so cosy and familiar. A colleague, who we will call Sam, tells this story which illustrates the point well.

Over the last ten years I have been working on my self-development: going to workshops; practising meditation; improving my communication skills and doing anything which I thought would help me to improve my life. During these ten years I have been married and divorced twice, having a child with each partner. Both the marriages went the same way, I spent hours each day in violent conflict with both women and in the end they left me. I just couldn't understand why these relationships were so angry and noisy when I so much wanted peace and calm in my life. I read somewhere that we are naturally inclined to repeat scenarios from our babyhood and this indeed was where the root of my problem lay. My parents had a turbulent and violent marriage (which they still have!). Although the logical and reasonable part of me wanted a loving and harmonious relationship there was a part of me that craved a repetition of the conflict of my babyhood. We love what we know and what is secure, and if turbulence rocked our cradle then we might crave to repeat it. Certainly I attracted two women who would give me a good fight and it's interesting to note that none of my previous girlfriends had shown this tendency. I looked for marriage partners who would help me to create what I understood marriage to mean at a very deep level. It took me a long time to work on my negative patterns in this area, I didn't change overnight. I have kept away from women who used to seem attractive to me and I am still finding it hard.

So, sometimes we unearth negative patterns which take some shifting, but of course *we can always change*. Negative behaviour can sometimes be like an addiction and we all know how hard it can be to break obsessive behaviour patterns, *but we can do it!* If you are facing problems which seem too great to bear then tackle smaller issues first. For example, if you were rejected as a child, you will be feeling the effects in many areas of your life. If you haven't the strength to tackle this at the moment then the time is not right for you. Know that, when you have the desire to look at this issue you will find the energy and support that you will need. This applies to all of you who are facing what feels like insurmountable difficulties: you will find the motivation to change when the time is right. Meanwhile, keep working on the creative visualization exercises and the spiritual practices. Don't let your major worries become a stumbling block for you, just step over them and get to work on your action plans. I have seen some amazing results when people work around the periphery of a problem instead of facing it directly. This often happens when we work on our self-respect and self-image and then suddenly that huge and terrifying problem starts to look less threatening.

There is another common reason why we sometimes fear change; we are afraid to rock the boat. I know that we have touched on this topic before, but it really is worth a revisit at this point. We have all got stories to tell about what happened when we changed, or what happened when we didn't change, and this is one of mine.

My first marriage was a bit of a disaster. As my husband began a new business venture I had two babies, close together in age, and naturally fell into a domestic role at home, whilst my husband became absorbed in his new project. As all mothers know, the new role is demanding, unknown, often terrifying, definitely mind-numbing a lot of the time, exhausting *all* of the time, as well as being one of the most amazing experiences on offer. Guilt and motherhood are so inextricably linked. The two together are an amazing emotional roller-coaster ride.

As my husband broadened his horizons mine seemed to become more and more narrow as I took my homespinning role very seriously. I started losing confidence in myself and began to tolerate behaviour which was unsupportive and eventually victimizing.

There were many times each day when I could have spoken up or acted differently and maybe saved that marriage: such retrospective wisdom! I chose to stay and embrace my victim role in a martyrish way; I was too afraid to demand changes and somehow I started to enjoy the role of the misunderstood wife and mother. What a price we pay when we turn away from our own truth and live the life of the poor victim. Of course, it eventually all blew up, or rather I did, and then I left with my two young children. And that *really* rocked the boat, which bobbed about dangerously for a number of years before I managed to pull myself together. And, as they say, the rest is history!

I know this isn't an unusual story; in fact, it's very common. Looking back I can see my part in creating this scenario (although at the time I was convinced it was all my husband's fault). I let myself down by being afraid to embrace change; to act on my intuition and to be the person I knew I really was. After the traumatic breakdown of that marriage and all the subsequent problems, I have never allowed myself to duck and dive away from facing up to challenges. Make changes when you need to or your worst fears will be realized, when you go on to create the realities of your nightmares rather than of your dreams.

TASK 28 ....

The Best That Can Happen

Think of something that you want to change but it feels too difficult. Write the answers in your journal.

I want to change . . . .

I am afraid to make changes because . . . .

Now answer these questions:

What is the worst thing that can happen to me if I make the change?

What is the best thing that can happen to me if I make the change?

How realistic are your answers? Will the world really fall apart if you start being more assertive? So what if some people would rather keep the old submissive you? True friends will always support your growth and development. What would be the benefits to you if you could ask for what you want? Check those unrealistic fears against the positive gains you will make and then just go ahead and do it!

The Leap of Faith

Whenever we get the urge to do something differently, to create something fresh, to initiate a change, there comes a moment when we have to take a chance. Luck is something that happens to us when we invite it to: we trigger synchronicity with a change in consciousness and we do this by being prepared to take the chance, by taking the risk. Significant changes always involve risk-taking; if there is no 'what if?' there can be no meaningful transformation. If you are looking for a major change in lifestyle then you must be prepared to take a leap of faith; and this is how you do it.

You must be committed. There can be no half-measures. If you think you *might like* a new job or getting fit *sounds like a good idea* or it *might be nice* to move house or start a new relationship or *you should* or *ought to* stop smoking, change your job ... then you can just forget it. You *must* be moved by a passionate desire in order to provide the forceful impulse which will trigger the energy needed to create the change. Have you ever noticed that happy and successful people have one outstanding feature in common? They are *passionate* about what they do; they are wholeheartedly committed to their endeavours; they are in love with their life. So, if you haven't got the passion you can't even leave first base; you will never have the strength of purpose to follow through. Don't be dismayed by this, you can learn to become full of the desire to succeed (more of this later).

You must take risks. Change is a risky business and it is fear of taking risks that has held you back until now. You might be afraid that you will look a fool (what if it all goes wrong?), or that others might reject you (who does she think she is, pushing herself forward in that way?), or that you are bound to fail (I don't deserve such happiness). You need to know that *everyone* who has ever done anything meaningful in their lives has had to face and overcome their own inhibiting demons. We all struggle with fears about what others will think, making mistakes, not being worthy of success ... until we make a commitment to ourselves. If we want to change the quality of our lives we must be prepared to stand up for ourselves. The most amazing things happen when you decide to believe in yourself: others start to demonstrate their belief in you, the universe responds to your thoughts, beliefs and emotions and as soon as you are prepared to move that one step forward, invisible forces will give you the strength to make a quantum leap. Try it!

You must go where the energy takes you. You are fuelled with a passionate desire; you have taken the first important step towards your goal and new doors are beginning to open. *You must go through these doors!* Don't dilly dally at the entrance, go forward with belief and conviction. At the threshold of these doors of opportunity you will meet the old negative beliefs, ideas, patterns, comfort zones etc. that have kept you in place all these years. The power of your commitment and your great desire to change will allow you to overcome these obstacles. Feel the new energy as it sweeps away the past. Go through your portals of opportunity and embrace your new realities.

Boldness Has Power and Magic in It

If your commitment is still wavering then you need to pep up your passion quotient. It's no good blowing hot and cold, you must be fired with enthusiasm and energy. Fear of commitment creates a halfhearted approach and only a wholehearted determination will succeed. Again we are looking at the framework of love as opposed to the framework of fear. When you look disbelievingly, through a negative filter, it's like driving with a dirty windscreen. Get those wipers going, clear the view, clarify your purpose. When you focus your laser beam of intent upon your goal your clear visualization magnetizes the physical energy needed to bring your goal into physical form. We can talk for ever about the need to be passionate and determined, but logical discussion does not necessarily bring results. Power and magic are at your fingertips; try the visualization in Task 29 and experience them.

TASK 29 ....

Transforming Energy

Stand up, legs slightly apart, arms opened wide and eyes closed. Visualize the life force entering through the crown of your head; imagine a shaft of white light passing into you. Feel the spiritual energy of the universe passing down through your throat and heart area, feel the expansion of energy here. As the white light passes through your arms and into your hands, you can feel spiritual energy reaching out into the world and magnetizing your material reality. Follow this spiritual/physical energy as it passes through your body and down through your legs; feel the activation and purpose it brings. Now your body is filled with white light and as you radiate this energy you become a shining star. Feel the power and magic within and without. Radiate pure energy and attract crystalline vision. You have the power!

....

Letting Joy into Your Life

Imagine this: you are standing at an intersection and one route is the path to struggle and one is the path to joy. You can choose which to take. Joy and struggle are not the result of things happening to you, they are attitudes, filters, approaches, frameworks, and you are always free to choose. Why come from fear when you can come from love? Why look at the mud when you can look at the stars? Why expect the worst when you can expect the best? Why choose to be a victim when you can create your own realities? Why be miserable when you can be happy? Give up the struggle, just for today. Just for today try the path of joy. Suspend all disbelief, fear and cynicism and let joy into your life. Take your joyful consciousness out into the world and smile. Stay in the moment, no dwelling in past problems or future fears and keep looking for the joyful path. When someone complains, recognize the path of struggle. If someone treats you badly, don't go down their path; turn the other cheek instead. Don't be distracted by the emotions and actions of others; keep in your calm and joyful centre. Do this for one day and see how it works. Don't be trapped by your thoughts and fears; choose to be uplifted instead. Every time you radiate joy you attract it back to you in even greater measure. Who knows, one joyful day might just lead to another.

TASK 30 ....

Your Love List

Take your journal and number the lines on the page from 1 to 30. Now begin. Make a list of everything that you love. Include people, food, music, hobbies, sensations, memories ... Here are a few things that come to mind for me: the walnut tree in my garden; the smell of lavender; my granddaughter's voice; my husband's smile; Marmite on toast; my computer; swimming; Belgian chocolates (well, *any* chocolates); daisies on the lawn; bookshops; Christmas; the family photos which cover the walls of my office; riding my red bike; apple crumble; picking strawberries; knitting; the smell of a cake cooking; sitting in the sunshine with a good book; hot baths; cosy winter evenings; my children's laughter; frost on the garden ... Can you see how things just keep coming? There is no limit here, go on and on if you want to, 30 was only a starting point. Open that door to joy and just see what lies ahead of you.

....

And So, One Step at a Time ...

Yes, you really can face your fears and do what you have to do. What is the worst that can happen to you? This is it, the time of your life. If you were to die tomorrow what would you wish to have done? Begin it today. Wherever you go you take yourself, there is no escape, so make sure you are the sort of person that you can spend a lifetime with. Be committed to your goals; trust the universe to guide your actions; take that leap of faith and be true to yourself; don't be afraid to take risks and go through your portals of opportunity when they arise. You have power and magic at your fingertips, radiate this energy and you will always attract all that you need. Stay in the moment and take the joyful path; live in love and you will love your life.

Key Points for Contemplation

1 You can always move into a positive cycle, if you really want to.

2 Negative behaviour can become addictive, but such obsessions can be broken.

3 Don't let your major worries become a stumbling block for you, just step over them and get to work on your action plans.

4 Rock the boat whilst the waves are small; don't wait until there is a major storm brewing.

5 True friends will always support your development and growth.

6 Luck enters our lives when we invite it to.

7 Significant changes always involve risk-taking.

8 Happy and successful people are passionate about their life.

9 Everyone who has ever done anything meaningful has had to face and overcome their inhibiting demons.

10 As soon as you are prepared to take that first step, invisible forces will give you the strength to make a quantum leap.

11 Go through the newly opening doors, sweep away the obstacles of the past.

12 Power and magic are at your fingertips, use them.

13 Radiate pure energy and attract crystalline vision. You have the power!

14 Why look at the mud when you can look at the stars?

15 Each time you radiate joy you attract it back in even greater measure.

16 Choose to be uplifted.

17 Stay in the moment and take the joyful path.

18 Wherever you go you take yourself, so become a joyful companion.

19 Live in love and you will love your life.

11

A New Self-Image

'As you reach the end of this sentence,
100,000 of your cells will have died —
you will be someone else.'

ROSS HEAVEN

All matter is energy, and you, me and the rest of the universe are in a constant state of flux. Spiritually, mentally, emotionally and physically we are continually on the move and so we can choose to change and recreate any aspect of ourselves in this or any other moment. But in the midst of life's uncertainties we like to hang on to some convictions and so we fashion various self-images which we project out into the world. Think about the roles you play: parent, worker (lots of possibilities here), cleaner, lover, driver, cinema-goer, shopper, client, partner, friend, cook, sister, brother, son, daughter, weight-lifter, gardener ... And now think about all the underlying patterns which have affected your role playing. What sort of messages have you internalized which help to create the images that you project today? If you were validated and emotionally supported as a child then you will find it easier to project an optimistic and hopeful image than if your family were critical and unsupportive. If creativity played an important part in your home life you are likely to consider your grown-up self as a creative person. If you come from a dysfunctional family where you had to play a watchful and caring role then this aspect of yourself will feature in your adult relationships. So here we are, a veritable mish-mash of culturally and parentally proscribed images; how can we know our true selves?

Who Do You Think You Are?

Are you kind, thoughtful, sensitive, rude, angry, beautiful, happy, miserable, supportive, amusing, stupid, clever, forgetful, critical, admiring, creative, non-creative, intelligent, skilful, perceptive, obtuse ...? And so it goes on, a never-ending list of possibilities and you can be all of these things some of the time. Human beings have the facility to feel any emotion, to think any thoughts and to act out any behaviour; all possibilities lie within us.

Some of our possible personalities might be hidden away from us, but if we can contact what Julia Cameron calls 'the jostling crowd of inner selves', then we can expand and develop in an amazing way. In psychological theory these inner selves have been called subpersonalities and they represent the different parts of our personality. Relax, this doesn't mean to suggest that we are all borderline schizophrenics. On the contrary, an awareness of our subpersonalities helps us to understand and resolve our inner conflicts. We can also think of subpersonalities as energy patterns: each facet of ourselves representing a different combination of spiritual, mental, emotional and physical energy.

I'm the Sort of Person Who ...

In your journal, make a list of what sort of person you think you are. Here are some examples from a client called Tony.

I'm the sort of person who: likes to be organized; is always punctual; always got good grades at school; is not very creative; doesn't have many original ideas; has high expectations of his relationships; likes his girlfriends to be neat and socially acceptable; doesn't like extrovert behaviour; is disappointed with the quality of his life; would like more excitement in his life; is frightened of change ...

This man has given a good thumbnail sketch of his self-image and you might feel, 'Ah yes, I know his type'. But do you? Even this short straightforward list demonstrates inner conflict. Tony runs a tight ship, with pretty rigid rules, and yet he would like more excitement in his life. He is frightened of change and so he sticks to the rules but he is disappointed with the way his life is turning out.

It doesn't take a doctorate in psychology to see one of Tony's underlying subpersonalities emerging from his list. He has a wild side which he is determinedly suppressing and this is creating inner conflict. He doesn't have to act out this wild subpersonality, he only needs to listen to its voice sometimes. When he's busy following his daily timetable he might suddenly feel bored and fed up. At this point 'wild' Tony might have a good idea and suggest that 'rigid' Tony does something outrageously different for once. This actually did happen with Tony and, as he gave his wilder side a voice, he began to introduce more balance and flexibility into his life.

Now, how about your list? If you are finding it hard to get going, start with, *I'm the sort of person who always …*

Sometimes we are busy suppressing certain subpersonalities because we are afraid that if we give them their head we will lose control of our lives and will become a crazy person. But the opposite is true. You are much more than you think you are; bring together your subpersonalities and your personality and self-image will become enriched.

Becoming Congruent

Perhaps you are still not convinced that you are a person of so many parts. Another way of understanding this is to think about a time when you felt inner doubt and conflict over an issue. Imagine that you have been offered an exciting career opportunity but for the last few years you have been dedicating your days to caring for your small children. A part of you, the carer and nurturer wants to stay at home, whilst the independence-loving and outgoing part of you would love to take the job. Inner conflict between our subpersonalities (particular patterns of energy) occurs when we don't allow them an airing. We resolve our inner conflicts by listening to the voices of these subpersonalities. In this example you could recognize that you are drawn to both possible outcomes and so you could weigh up the pros and cons and come to some resolution.

Congruence derives from the Latin word *congruere*, which means to meet together and to agree. Congruence happens when all your subpersonalities come together in harmony to create an agreed outcome; all 'parts' of you are happy and you feel whole and balanced. When you feel guilty, discontented, unhappy, angry, dissatisfied, fearful, out of control, depressed or any other negative condition that you can imagine, just stop and think about where you are out of balance. Which part of your personality is being ignored? Which inner voice isn't being heard? Which energy pattern is trying to capture your attention? Don't let your old images of yourself (past roles, expectations and patterning) define you. Embrace and love all parts of yourself (especially what you consider to be the negative aspects) and your self-image will become richer, positive, and more expansive than you could have dreamed possible.

Discovering New Self-Images

Go back to your *I'm the sort of person who ...* list. Look particularly at anything on your *I'm the sort of person who always ...* list. Consider any of these images of yourself which suggest rigidity and inflexibility. It is unrealistic to think that you are *always* going to behave, think, feel and act in a certain way. The universe is changing at every moment and so are you. Welcome this knowledge and open yourself to the possibility of new inner awareness. Which aspects of your self-image are holding you back? How would you like to demonstrate some different personality traits? Which new self-images would you like to project into the world? Have you any fantasy selves sitting around in your imagination? One respected businessman I know realized a lifelong desire when he formed a band and changed his suit in the evening to play rock and roll in a local club. A woman who works in a library became a weightlifting champion and a colleague has just started tap-dancing lessons at the age of 54. Your fantasy selves can stay in your imagination (you don't have to act them out), but do become aware of them; they are a part of you. If you deny that you have dreams and shut away the parts of you that you feel are unacceptable, they will one day burst out from hiding. Think how often people turn their lives upside down when they reach their middle years. We say they are suffering a mid-life crisis, but we could interpret this behaviour as a response and reaction to the unfulfilled dreams and desires that they have suppressed throughout their lives.

Your Higher Self

So many amazing roles we can play, such rich experiences to be had and yet we might still feel dissatisfied. Why should this be? What else could be missing? You might be projecting upbeat and decisive self-images; you may be fulfilling many dreams and radiating and attracting positive energy and *it still might not be enough!* Self-image is all about personality. Imagine entering the wardrobe department of your life and choosing a costume of one of your personalities. We 'wear' our personalities just like costumes in a play and the action is set in the material world. Beyond the dramas and the roles we play is something more, and it is this that tells us who we *really* are.

Yes, you may be a mother, daughter, office worker, lover, cook, dog-walker and even tap-dancer and rock and roller ... but you are also something else. Above and beyond your incredible gang of inner selves is your Higher Self, also sometimes called the True or the Authentic Self. Your Higher Self is the part of you which is connected to the divine spark of consciousness shared by all living things. You are in contact with your Higher Self whenever you are operating at the spiritual level. Your Higher Self loves you unconditionally and helps you to get to know and to evolve your subpersonalities, so that they become aligned with your higher purpose. You are divine, you are spiritual and you are here to realize your amazing potential; this is your true purpose. As you develop a greater self-awareness and begin to recognize and evolve your subpersonalities you will feel yourself becoming lighter and freer. As your inner selves begin to work together you will feel more energized and alive. Always remember that you can look beyond your current self-images to your Higher Self; the part of you which transcends your personality and holds the essence of who you really are.

Creating Realities with Our Images of Ourselves

Some of the roles we play and the self-images we project have developed from energy patterns which are light, positive, life-affirming and creative. Such roles and self-images work for us and give us the self-esteem and self-respect that we need to make the very most of our lives. When we are true to ourselves our self-images reflect this. Others 'pick up' whatever energetic vibration we are radiating, and strong and positive self-images have a powerful effect on the sort of realities that we can create. When we project self-confidence we immediately enter a positive spiral: we feel good about ourselves; we expect the best to happen (and so we attract it); our confidence increases as we create a positive self-fulfilling prophecy, and life feels good. We need to take a look at the roles we play, the self-images we hold and the beliefs and patterns that support them. Your definition of yourself will have a great influence on your behaviour: the type of person you think you are will determine which of two paths you can take. You can choose to live either as a victim, who can only react to what happens to her, or as a person who consciously creates her own reality. If you choose to live creatively then your self-images and the roles you play must project energy which is positive, enthusiastic, motivated, risk-taking, reflective and self-aware.

Let's move on now to the action planning section of this chapter. Here we bring together various techniques and approaches which will guide you to create a personal action plan for improving your self-image and enhancing your life.

YOUR PERSONAL ACTION PLAN
FOR CREATING A NEW SELF-IMAGE

First let's go back to your Life Zone Assessment (Task 16, page 77). Look at how you answered the questions on self-image. And now answer them again in your journal. As you are working through this book you might already be feeling that you are beginning to change. Your answers may be different this time around or they might be the same.

Reassessment of Self-Image Life Zone

My present satisfaction level is ...

I am happy/unhappy with this score ...

The words I use to describe myself are ...

When I reflect on my self-image I feel ...

I believe that I am ...

My hopes and fears about the way I see myself are ...

Your Attitudes to Your Self-Image

Underlying your answers are the thought, feeling and behaviour patterns which run your life. Your definitions of yourself (kind, creative, stupid, clever, sensitive, clumsy, thoughtful, pessimistic or whatever) are based in your self-belief. Go back to Task 9 on page 34 and look at your responses. Now let's repeat this exercise, to see if your answers have changed and to look at them in greater depth.

Self-Image Review

What do you believe to be true about yourself? Read the following list (adding any other adjectives you wish) and put the words *I am* before each word. Score as follows: 0 – almost never; 1 – sometimes; 2 – often; 3 – almost always.

rigid	spontaneous	guilty	intuitive	embarrassed
reflective	controlled	sensitive	boring	irritable
worthy	joyful	self-conscious	proud	critical
free	caring	predictable	tolerant	articulate
interesting	depressed	worthless	loveable	adventurous
kind	shy	bossy	negative	lazy
confident	helpless	fearful	capable	flexible
protective	passive	optimistic	happy	temperamental
indecisive	exciting	stupid	self-aware	foolish
cynical	intelligent	trustworthy	supportive	amusing

Have any of your answers changed? Look at where you scored 3. What do you think that you are almost always?

I am almost always . . . .

How do these aspects of your self-image affect your life? For example, if you think that you are almost always worthless, then you will see yourself as a victim and your lack of self-esteem will attract 'bad luck' and poor relationships. On the other hand, if you consider that you are almost always optimistic then you will project a more light hearted and approachable image, which will attract new prospects and relationships. The big question is, which of these characteristics work for you and which don't?

Would you like to change any of your *almost always* characteristics? What would you like to change?

I would like to change . . . .

Now, where did you score 0? What do you think that you are almost never?

I am almost never . . . .

Does the lack of any of these features have a detrimental effect on the way your life is running? If so, can you be specific about these effects?

The qualities I lack create the following limitations for me . . . .

. . . .

What, if any of your *almost never* characteristics would you like to include in your self-image? For example, if you think that you are almost never adventurous, you will find it hard to take risks and to move forward in any of your life zones. Learning to face your fears, to have faith in yourself and to take that risky first step would be a way to include an adventurous aspect in your self-image.

I would like to include the following qualities in my self-image . . . . . .

. . . .

List eight adjectives that best describe you.

I am . . . .

Now, from this thumbnail sketch choose the statement which you feel is most important. This is your core belief and it underpins and creates all aspects of your self-image.

My core belief is that I am . . . .

And what does this statement reveal to you? Is it positively self-affirming or is it self-critical?

Now think long and hard about all your positive qualities. Don't be shy, this is not the time to be self-effacing. Go on, be nice to yourself. Imagine that you are someone else looking at you; what good things can you see?

I like the fact that I . . . .

I am proud of myself for . . . .

My skills and strengths are . . . .

I love being myself when I . . . .

I feel great when I am . . . .

The best moment of my life was when I . . . .

Create as many of these statements as you can. Forget about, 'not bragging' and 'not pushing yourself forward'. I want you to *really show off*; just how amazing can you let yourself be?

Our self-image exactly reflects our self-beliefs. We know that beliefs can be changed, and so we are always free to create a new self-image which is in harmony with our real needs.

Setting New Goals

Our intention and desires are the finest energy movers and new reality creators that we possess. Be ready now to specify your intentions. What is it that you would most like to change about yourself? Reflect on all the questions you have already answered in this action plan and make your decisions. Think about your short-term goals (achievable in under three months) and your longer-term goals.

Write down your goals (this is very empowering). Here are some examples of possible goals:

Short term

To be more assertive.

To say what I mean.

To become more appreciative and positive.

To be prepared to take some risks.

To allow myself to be happy and joyful.

Long term

To develop my creative side.

To improve my levels of skill.

To learn to love and appreciate myself.

To be able to forgive and let go of my resentments.

To overcome my physical fears.

If you can't ask for what you want, how can you ever expect it to manifest? If you don't set goals you will never be able to measure your achievements. So write them down. Now, how much do you want to achieve your goals? How strong is your desire? If you just think 'it might be nice' or 'you would quite like to', then, as I said earlier, you had better forget all about it. You must be *entirely passionate and committed* to your goals. You must be prepared to give it all it takes. The journey from dream to reality takes focus and determination. These qualities galvanize the energy needed to turn your vision into actuality.

Realizing Your Goals

Accomplishment will only occur when all 'parts' of our energy are flowing together in harmony. Balance and equilibrium create the optimum conditions for the realization of our goals. We need to work at all levels of our being: mental, spiritual, emotional and physical.

Achieving your new self-image goals

Thought creates form is one of the 4 Principles of Creativity. And the following expression (which we looked at on page 21), demonstrates how this creative process occurs.

THOUGHT ENERGY	X	EMOTIONAL ENERGY	>	MATERIAL ENERGY

Getting what you want, whether it's a new car or a change of self-image, depends upon belief, vision, commitment and action. Nothing can change for you unless you can imagine that it will; your belief must be total. Your accompanying visions (of how the changes will manifest) must support your belief, and then the required physical energy will be enabled to create the changes.

So we need to take a holistic approach to creating and realizing our goals. This will mean changing our mental, spiritual, emotional and physical energy.

Your mental energy

This is our mind energy and includes all our thoughts, ideas and beliefs. We have discussed this energy in great detail, and I'm sure that it will come as no surprise to you to learn that all change starts here, with an idea. Go back and review any beliefs and self-images that might obstruct the realization of your goals. For example, if one of your goals was 'To say what I mean', and one of your beliefs (and part of your self-image) is that 'I am a poor communicator', then obviously this negative affirmation must be changed.

Make a list of any aspects of your self-belief and self-image which could prevent you from achieving your goals.

Aspects of my self-belief and self-image which could stop me realizing my goals ...

Now take this list of negative affirmations and turn them around. The following example shows how to do this.

Negative affirmation	(changes to) Positive affirmation
I am a poor communicator	I am a good communicator
I am a loser	I am a winner
I am not clever enough	I am good enough

I always make mistakes	I give things my best shot
I am stuck	I am changing
I am alone	The universe supports me
No one cares what I do	My contribution is important
I can never fit in	I am unique

I'm sure that you get the idea. Remember to keep your affirmations positive and in the present tense (if you affirm that you 'will be' something, it will always stay there, in the future). Concentrate on what you want more of rather than what you want less of (what you put your attention on grows). So, rather than say, 'I want to be less negative', you would say, 'I am positive'. Make it real, make it happen in this very moment.

Your spiritual energy

If they are to work, positive affirmations must be supported by positive visions. And here you put your spiritual energy to work by looking inside yourself and creatively visualizing the realization of your goals.

Get into a relaxed state and see, feel and experience yourself making your dreams come true. If you want to be more successful, see yourself flourishing, hear the admiration of others, be specific and fill in all the details (how will your success manifest?). Really experience your success in full Technicolor; feel what it is like to be the person you would most like to be. Let your positive visualizations replace all those old pictures of yourself that didn't work for you.

NEGATIVE AFFIRMATIONS	+	NEGATIVE VISUALIZATIONS	→	OLD NEGATIVE REALITIES
POSITIVE AFFIRMATIONS	+	POSITIVE REALITIES	→	NEW CHANGED VISUALIZATIONS

Your emotional energy

We attract whatever we radiate. The strength of our beliefs and expectations together with the power of our imagination come together and and attract into our lives the energy that we are radiating. Clarity of purpose is driven by the intensity of our motivation and desire. If you cannot raise the passion required to achieve your goals then there is no point even trying. The desire to change your self-image must be powerful. The difference between the person who makes things happen and the person who has things happen to her can be found in her motivation. If you are not hungry enough to gather your commitment and push through the changes you will remain a victim of circumstance. So, just how hungry are you? When you look at your self-image do you feel a lukewarm response to change or are you driven by a burning urge to create a new you?

If you are still held back by indifference then maybe this means that it is not the right time for you to make changes. On the other hand, it might be worth digging a little deeper into your emotional energy to see if there are any feelings that could be limiting you. Look back over all your responses to the questions in this action plan. Reflect on your feelings as you look at your answers. Is there a block in your emotional energy? Are you in touch with your feelings and are you able to express them? Muddled and unexpressed emotions can prevent the clarity we need to become self-motivated. Are there things that you would like to say but find it hard to? If so, write them in your journal.

I would like to say that ...

Who would you like to say these things to?
I would like to tell ... that I am feeling ...

Do you need to admit some feelings to yourself that you have been unable to before? If so, what are they?
I am feeling ...

Investigate your feelings to see if you have any blockages in your emotional energy. You can let go of unexpressed feelings in any number of ways: by admitting them to yourself; expressing them to someone else; writing them down; having a good shout/weep; banging pillows ... Try some of these techniques if your levels of passionate intent have dropped through the floor. As you clear your backlog of hidden emotions and bring your feelings out for an airing, you will find that your energy levels will increase and your motivation levels will rise. When you can drum up enough energy to create a laser beam of focused desire for your outcome – that outcome is assured.

Your physical energy

New positive affirmations and visualizations, fired with the enthusiasm of total commitment, will generate the action needed to create the new outcome. Action never stands alone, it is always the end result of a process which involves various patterns of energy, including beliefs, visualizations, expectations, thoughts, imaginings and emotions. Our behaviour patterns are a reflection of the ways we think and feel about ourselves and our world.

Remember those two frameworks around which we can choose to create our personal realities. Will you choose love or fear; expansion or limitation; positivity or negativity? Will you choose the path of conscious creativity or the path of reactive victim behaviour?

If you see yourself as a victim, then you will never be able to get a meaningful grip on your life. Decisions will not be carried to a conclusion; you will always be someone's doormat; something will always stop you from reaching your goal and this will always be someone else's fault.

Creative behaviour requires a trusting, questing, open-hearted approach and comes from a sense of personal responsibility; there is no one to blame, we create our own life circumstances, the ball is always in our court.

Victim consciousness changes to creative consciousness when we change the way we act and begin to behave assertively. Assertive behaviour requires that we know what we want, respect ourselves and others, take full responsibility for our actions, use good, clear communication skills, are prepared to take a risk or two and are willing to express our true feelings. One good, simple and truly effective way to develop assertion techniques is to learn to say 'no' when we want to. This might be a little word but it packs a big punch and can take you instantaneously from the doormat, across the threshold and into a new reality. Work on being assertive and your new self-respect will magically transform your self-image. You *can* ask for what you want and you *can* get what you want if you are a good and clear communicator: it's not just *what* you do, it's the *way that you do it* that counts!

For a New Self-Image

- Work at all levels of your being and use any of the techniques in this book that will help you.

- Let yourself become aware of the many transitory roles you play and the self-images that you project.

- Appreciate the fact that you can always change your self-image so that it will support your new visions and realities.

- Remember that you have the ability to look beyond the image of yourself to contact that part of you which is spiritual, divine, loving and all knowing.

- Transcend your personality selves. Lift above your self-images to contact your Higher Self, and you will be able to feel the essence of who you *really* are.

12

Creating Amazing Relationships

'My true relationship is my relationship with myself — all others are simply mirrors of it.'

If I could just get my social life together I'd be so much more confident. If only I could find the perfect partner, I know my life would feel complete. If my parents would just stop criticizing my lifestyle, I would feel free to be me. Oh, if only I could just change everybody, I would be so happy.

Reflect upon your love life, your family connections and your friendships. Who or what would you like to transform to improve the quality of all of your relationships? Make a list in your journal, name names, and specify the ways that you would like to see each person change.

But even if you had a magic wand, it couldn't work, because it is a hopeless task to try to change anybody. A frog will only change into a prince in a fairy tale. An alcoholic will only stop drinking if he chooses to. A lover will only stop cheating on you when he decides to change his ways. A friend will only support you if she feels like it. Your children will only treat you with the amount of respect that they think you deserve. Every moment spent waiting for someone to change is a waste of time. If your happiness depends on the way that others behave, then you have lost direction and become a victim.

We *can* transform our relationships, but only if we change our focus from the *outside* to the *inside*. Relationships are made within us, and here lies the true magic.

The Magic of Relationships

Lovers, family and friends; three separate worlds – or are they? Whatever can be the connection between your awful ex, the family member who drives you to distraction, your latest love interest who has turned out to be such a bore, that friend who keeps letting you down ...? Why, *you* are that connection, of course.

The 4 Principles of Creativity tell us that because the universe is pure energy, our energy is magnetic; form follows thought; we will attract whatever we radiate; our awareness of energy raises our vibration. In other words, we create whatever it is that we think about: our thoughts create our reality; we get what we expect to get and what we think we deserve.

The magic inherent in all our relationships lies in their capacity to *mirror exactly* our own inner processes. There is nothing haphazard about the way we run our lives: events and situations don't 'just happen' to us (even if we sometimes like to think so when things go wrong). We do indeed create the personal realities of our lives by magnetizing people and circumstances with the radiations of our own personal energy. It is easy to accept that we create our own relationships when our lives are going well (we have attracted a fabulous new partner, made a good friend, are at peace with our family), and much harder to accept this responsibility when our relationships are not working. When you are at crisis point with your partner, when a friend is unkind, when your father is irritating you beyond endurance, how can these situations be of your own making? Why would you attract discord into your life?

We can begin to understand why as soon as we transform the way we view our relationships. Instead of looking at others to provide the fulfilment we need to make our lives feel complete, we are going to look inside at ourselves. *The biggest and most important relationship you will ever have is the one that you are having with yourself; all your other relationships are simply reflections of this one.*

Relationships as Mirrors

We attract to ourselves what we most need to learn. This is the way we develop and grow towards realizing our full human potential. Throughout this book we have seen numerous examples of this process in action: our personal challenges continually moving us onward as we learn to overcome obstacles and develop and integrate new aspects of ourselves.

The ways that people treat us are a reflection of the ways that we treat ourselves, and so *all* our relationships (even those that feel like 'failures') can tell us a lot about our own process.

If my self-esteem is high, then I will attract the respect of others: people will treat me well because I value myself. When I have developed my spirituality I can appreciate and love my life and this energy attracts others who are also light-hearted and loving. As I learn to stop criticizing myself, my relationships will become more supportive. If I am filled with guilt then I will experience lack of forgiveness in others. When I am holding anger and resentment I will magnetize angry and resentful people into my life. And so you can see that this mirroring effect can be used as an amazing tool for self-development. Instead of looking outside ourselves and blaming others for our poor relationships, we can stop and answer these two questions.

1 What is this relationship showing me about myself?

2 How can I use this insight to improve the quality of the relationships that I attract?

Remember that:

- our inner selves (thoughts, beliefs, emotions, expectations ...) create the nature of all of our relationships.

- these relationships can then reveal to us new ways of looking at ourselves.

- this knowledge shows us how to create new, improved relationships.

Using the Process

We magnetize people into our orbit and invite them into our lives. But why would we choose to surround ourselves with difficult people whom we would never consciously wish to attract?

Case study

Lisa is in her late twenties, holds down a powerful job and knows how to be assertive in the workplace but she falls apart in the love department. This is how she describes her emotional life:

> It's an absolute nightmare, I can never make good decisions in my love life. The men I choose always end up making me feel useless. I do everything I can to make my relationships work; I'm kind and thoughtful and nothing is ever too much trouble for me; I always support the men in my life. Why do men continually treat me badly? I think they're all selfish and that they're only interested in their own needs.

Why does Lisa keep having relationships with men who treat her badly? Is it because all men are selfish? Of course not, this is just a belief that she holds which she keeps reinforcing by going for the men who will treat her like a victim. She does in fact admit that she makes poor decisions about men. Lisa keeps repeating the same old behaviour patterns by looking for the same 'type' of man. Her patterns (thoughts, feelings, behaviours) are attracting men whose own patterns are uncaring and victimizing.

We will keep repeating our unfulfilling patterns until we decide to change them and we are unable to make this decision until we become conscious that *something needs to change*. And this is why our understanding of the process of relationships as mirrors is so fascinating and so useful. The quality of our relationships tells us where we are at! We are constantly creating the drama of our lives; we choose the stage, the props and the cast. What sort of play are you directing? Look at your relationships and ask yourself, 'What am I creating here?' and then, most importantly, 'What do these relationships tell me about myself?'

Our relationships demonstrate a powerful and exact reflection of our own personal development.

Lisa attracts men who don't treat her with respect. These men mistreat her, but only because she allows them to. Why does she choose such characters? What does this type of relationship say about her?

At some level Lisa believes that she deserves to be victimized; if she didn't she would never allow anyone to treat her badly. Her poor relationships have repeated over and over until at last she is able to see what is happening to her. The amazing truth is that we attract into our lives whatever we need to learn in order to develop and grow and become whole. We do this by bringing into our personal cast all the people who *exactly* reflect the lessons we need to work on. In this way we can see that our relationships are mirrors of ourselves; a truly amazing and magical process. Even though our repeating patterns may be creating a negative outcome (as Lisa continually experienced victimization by men), we cannot change these patterns until we recognize what we are creating. And so, we can identify our own patterns by focusing on the exact nature of our relationships, because these hold all the clues we need to develop and grow.

Of course, all of your associations will be completely different: each relationship is a unique blend of all the patterns that the participants bring to it. However, *all your relationships begin with you.* The most important relationship that you will ever have in this life is the relationship you have with yourself; all the rest are merely a reflection of this one. As you are creating your own relationships you can choose which types to attract. Will they be supportive and appreciative or will they be critical and victimizing? Will you use the reflecting process within your relationships to help you to change and move on, or will you just allow yourself to keep repeating negative patterns by blaming everyone else?

Checking Your Boundaries

How close do you get to people? I was once giving a talk on relationships and chose four people at random to pair off. Because there were a lot of people in the lecture hall and because I had chosen people who were not sitting anywhere near each other, I assumed that the couples were strangers to each other. Both couples stood some distance apart and then I asked them to walk towards each other. I was using this little experiment to show how we naturally create physical boundaries with each other. One pair stopped about a metre apart whilst the other pair embraced each other. Would you believe it? My random selection had chosen a pair of sisters! None of us was expecting such closeness, but almost immediately it happened we all assumed that the couple knew each other very well. This demonstration proved the point nicely: we create physical boundaries in all our relationships and they differ according to emotional closeness. So, whilst you might happily kiss and hug a family member you would probably keep your distance with a work colleague.

A healthy relationship is defined as one that allows us to satisfy our basic needs, and a useful way to recognize these needs is to become aware of our personal boundaries. The boundaries, or limits we set, reflect the distance we are prepared to go within a relationship and they exist beyond the physical level. We set mental, spiritual and emotional boundaries as well as the more obvious physical ones. As soon as we become aware of our boundaries we gain an insight into who we are and what we want from our relationships. Until we know this we will be unable to have a healthy relationship, whether it is casual, close or intimate.

Imagine that you are meeting someone for the first time. Your (invisible) boundaries are intact and there is physical space between you. As you get to know each other you begin to share ideas, feelings and experiences and so there is a shared space between you. Your boundaries remain intact, you both still have a strong sense of personal identity and this is a healthy relationship (both sets of needs are being met). If you ever lose sight of your own personal limits then your boundaries have blurred into each other and the relationship is described as unhealthy: neither of you has a true sense of self any more. Becoming close and intimate does not require that you lose yourself in another person: the loss of self always means the loss of a good, healthy relationship. We have all experienced an invasion of our personal boundaries and it doesn't feel good.

You will know whenever your relationship boundaries become blurred because you will be troubled by such internal dilemmas as: Do I want this or am I doing it because you want to? I can't tell what I really think. Can I trust my own judgement? Where do I end and you begin? I can't seem to make any clear decisions. How much are you influencing me?

In the following action plan we will use the mirroring process and personal boundary checks, to evaluate where we stand in all of our relationships. We will only be able to establish new relationship goals when we can bring personal clarity and self-awareness to our friendships, love lives and family connections. As soon as we know what we want from our relationships we attract the people who can reflect these needs. Low self-confidence and blurred boundaries invite victimizers, criticizers and abusers into our lives. A strong sense of self-worth and self-respect will create strong healthy boundaries and will attract people who will be positive mirrors for us; they will be supportive and validating.

Why not choose to create amazing relationships?

YOUR PERSONAL ACTION PLAN FOR IMPROVING ALL YOUR RELATIONSHIPS

Every single relationship that you have begins with you and reflects the relationship that you have with yourself. Make no mistake about this, you will find yourself (along with all your energy patterns) at the creative centre of *all* of your relationships. Because your relationships are all about you, as opposed to being about your lovers, family members and friends, this action plan will be focusing on you and not on them. You are attracting all the people who feature in your life drama; you are the connecting link. And so this action plan will help you to improve all of your relationships by learning how to change yourself. You can apply these techniques to any or all of your relationships and be sure of an improvement in all three of your life zones: Love, Family and Friends.

Refer to your Life Zone Assessments for all three of your relationship life zones. Make three separate reassessments for each zone and check your original answers against your reassessments. Perhaps you have already made some changes in perception.

Reassessment of Relationship Life Zone

Love

My present satisfaction level is ....

I am happy/unhappy with this score ....

I would describe my love life as ....

When I think about my intimate relationships I feel ....

I believe that love is ....

My hopes and fears about intimacy are ....

Family

My present satisfaction level is . . . .

I am happy/unhappy with this score . . . .

I would describe my relationships with the members of my family as

. . . .

When I think about the members of my family I feel . . . .

I believe that families are . . . .

My hopes and fears for my family relationships are .. . .

. . . .

Friends

My present satisfaction level is . . . .

I am happy/unhappy with this score . . . .

I would describe my social life as . . . .

When I think about my friendships I feel . . . .

I believe that friendship is . . . .

My hopes and fears for my friendships are . . . .

I know that some of you will be reeling with the sheer numbers of people that you are trying to deal with here. At first, just choose a few key figures and typical problem areas to work with, and some clear patterns will begin to emerge.

Your Attitudes to Your Relationships

Remember that whatever relationships we attract will always reflect our own beliefs or qualities in some way. You might disagree. How could that judgemental, critical and thoughtless woman be reflecting something within me? I'm not unkind! And how is it possible that I have drawn such an angry and hard man into my life? I'm not like him, I never show my anger! Try the following and put your answers into your journal.

1 Think of three people in your life who get on your nerves. Name them.

2 Now think of three things that you don't like about each of these people and that you would like them to change.

3 Now comes the hard bit. Look inside and ask yourself:

How am I like this?

When do I act like they do?

This is a hard exercise and takes some soul-searching. If you can't find any ways that these three relationships are mirroring aspects of yourself then keep looking. Whenever we feel strong emotions about anyone we have an emotional hook with their energy: we are magnetic to them in some way. This is easy to believe when we are in a relationship that is going well and the emotional hooks all feel positive: he is so loving (yes, I'm like that); she is so kind and generous (yes, I'm like that too); he has always believed in me (yes, I am a positive mirror for others). But how about those emotional hooks that create irritation, anger, resentment, even hatred: he is abusing me (I'm not like that); they are always criticizing me (I'm not a critical person); she is like a walking volcano (I am never angry).

If you are in an abusive relationship, what is making you stay? Do you believe that you deserve this type of treatment? Do you believe that this is how relationships work because you have early childhood memories of abuse?

If you experience criticism from family members, lovers or friends then ask yourself this question. How do I bring myself down? In what ways do I criticize myself? Where do I think I am not good enough? If you think badly of yourself, others soon pick up that energy pattern and before you know it you are attracting all the bullies under the sun!

If you believe that some emotions are taboo and should never be mentioned or shown but always denied, then you have created a strong emotional hook with these feelings. It is possible for us all to experience the whole range of human emotions and if we suppress or deny any of our feelings then the universe will obligingly bring them into our lives via our relationships. And so, for example, a person who denies her anger will find herself surrounded by angry people (reflecting what she is denying). If there are angry people in your life, look deeply at your feelings. Are you being true to yourself? Where are you annoyed and resentful? Just accepting that you have denied these feelings is often enough to start the process of clearing this pattern.

Your beliefs about relationships

What are your beliefs and expectations about the nature of your relationships?

What did you learn about relationships from your parents?

How did they demonstrate their love, or didn't they?

How would you describe your parents' relationship when you were a child?

Did your parents have friends?

Did they encourage you to have friends?

Were you a close family?

Is your family close now?

Pursue the answers to these questions, however painful it feels. Remember the creative power of belief: you can only create the relationships that you believe are possible. *You deserve amazing relationships.*

Setting New Goals

As you have been reflecting on your love life, family relationships and friendships, I'm sure you are beginning to feel inspired to set some new relationship goals. Using all the information you have gathered so far, take a realistic look at all your relationships: what they are like now and how you would like them to improve. Remember that your goal cannot be to change someone else's behaviour; the focus for change is on you. Set out your goals in your journal, taking one zone at a time. Here are a few possible examples.

Love relationship goals

To make our relationship closer.

To feel like an equal partner.

To have more fun and excitement.

To be in a loving and supportive relationship.

To improve our sex life.

To have better communication with my partner.

Family relationship goals

To encourage everyone to say what they really mean.

To have more family get-togethers.

To hold back on my judgements and to learn to be more forgiving.

To remember that my parents could only teach me what they knew; they had parents, too.

To be more understanding and tolerant.

To give my children more time and attention.

Friendship goals

To expand my social life.

To increase my circle of friends.

To meet new people who have interests different from
mine.

To accept more invitations.

To allow myself to let my hair down once in a while.

Let your goals reflect the way you visualize your improved relationships.

Realizing Your Goals

In order to achieve your relationship goals you will need to be
prepared to dig deep inside yourself and to tell the truth about
your feelings. You do this by:

Checking out the reflective process by asking, what is this
relationship showing me about myself?

Checking your boundaries by asking, are my boundaries still
intact or are they becoming blurred; is this a healthy or
unhealthy relationship?
Look at the following checklist to see how strong and intact
your own boundaries are.

Personal boundary checklist

Answer the following questions, using these options:
- Almost never
- Sometimes
- Often
- Almost always

I am good at expressing my true feelings . . . .

Anger frightens me . . . .

I often feel used by others . . . .

I find it hard to keep secrets . . . .

I am afraid to stand up for myself . . . .

I trust myself . . . .

I make relationships with people who are not good for me . . . .

I feel a strong spiritual connection . . . .

I feel lost and alone . . . .

I feel miserable if others are miserable . . . .

I will do anything for a quiet life . . . .

I am a good judge of character . . . .

I feel wounded when I am criticized . . . .

I will not stay in an abusive relationship . . . .

I am very sensitive to the moods of others . . . .

I like to make others feel good . . . .

Think about how your answers might be affecting the quality of your relationships. Do any of your feelings or ways in which you behave make social interaction difficult? If so, these are the areas where your boundaries are weak. Whenever you have a relationship problem you need to check the strength of your boundaries. Look at your own behaviour and emotions; take responsibility for your own needs and remember that the best relationships are those where everyone is free to be themselves.

After you have used the reflective process, and checked your boundaries, you will become clearer about where you stand, and the part you play, in each of your relationships. Once this is established you will find it easier to achieve your goals.

For example, if you are in a relationship where someone is always blaming you and you apply the reflective process and check your boundaries, you might come to a surprising conclusion. He can only keep bringing you down if you agree to take the blame, and your boundaries are blurred if you aren't able to stand up for yourself. And so it becomes obvious that you will never be able to improve this relationship until you make a firm stand and refuse to take the blame. Your drastic change in behaviour can have two outcomes: either this person will stop blaming you, as you assert yourself, and the health of your relationship will improve, or the relationship will end. Sometimes we are sticking to old relationships even though they don't work any more. As you work towards your new relationship objectives you might find that you have outgrown some of your associations. This is fine! Move on if you have to, and attract positive and supportive relationships which help you to realize your goals.

Good family relationships require:

1 clarity (of the part you play),

2 commitment (to making them work at some level which is acceptable),

3 forgiveness (in large doses).

We are inclined to hurt most those who are closest to us and this often means our family members. Maybe you have discovered some negative patterns that you share with your parents (and how annoying this is, to see your own limiting beliefs reflected back to you!). And what about your children's irritating habits? You can be absolutely sure that at least half of them are yours! Use the reflective process with a liberal dose of forgiveness. You never can walk away from your family: the bonds remain, however far away you go.

Achieving your relationship goals

Take each of your goals and consider anything which might stand in the way of your success. Clarify your position by using the reflective process and by checking your boundaries. Have you any thought, feeling or behaviour patterns which are stopping you from creating the relationships you desire?

Your mental energy

Check how your beliefs might be affecting your love, family and friendship goals. Make some lists in your journal. Now take any negative belief and replace it with a positive affirmation. Some examples follow.

Old negative belief	New positive affirmation
I don't deserve to be loved	I deserve loving relationships
I am never good enough	I am good enough, just the way I am
My parents didn't show me love	My parents taught me all they knew; I can forgive them
My sister was the favourite	I appreciate and value myself
I was an isolated child	I welcome new friendships
I am afraid of intimacy	Intimate relationships are joyful
I don't spend enough time with my children	I give my children the best I can
I hang on to old hurts	Letting go is easy. I am free to change
I am always the victim	My personal boundaries are strong. I only have healthy relationships
I feel powerless in my relationships	I create my own relationships

You are a wonderful person and you deserve loving relationships, every time!

Your spiritual energy

The following fascinating exercise can have a really dramatic effect on a any relationship issue.

Go into a relaxed state and recreate your personal sanctuary (as you did on page 124). Visualize yourself in this beautiful place where you are free from all limitations. Sitting opposite you is the person with whom you are having difficulties at the moment; you have invited her to your sanctuary to talk things out. As you explain to her that you need to discuss some of your feelings, you realize that she is of the same mind. You both want to overcome your difficulties and are ready to listen carefully to what the other has to stay. As you start to appreciate each other's point of view, you realize that you both want to resolve your communication problem. When the meeting ends you embrace each other with new clarity and understanding. When you open your eyes and return from your sanctuary you know without a doubt that there has been an energetic shift in this relationship. Remember, we are all telepathic and at some level your friend knows exactly what has occurred between you. This is a brilliant technique, try it now!

Take your relationship goals and help activate them with creative visualization. Use the techniques you have used before to see, feel and experience your new goals in action.

Your emotional energy

I am sure that this action plan will have uncovered many emotions which you will need to work through in some way. Sometimes it really helps to speak your feelings out loud when you are alone. I often do this when I need to get something off my chest but it doesn't feel appropriate to tell anyone. Although it's considered to be the first sign of insanity, I think that talking to yourself is often a very sane move. Take those deep and personal feelings which are so hard to share and tell them to the universe. Amazing things happen when you do this. Don't take my word for it, try it and see.

Your physical energy

Take the following action for immediate results.

Be decisive and follow through with appropriate action. Communicate your needs clearly and walk away if your needs are not met. Don't be afraid to speak your mind, or you will let yourself down. Assert yourself, you are not a victim. Walk away from abuse. Forgive yourself, you are doing your best.

For New Improved Relationships

- Radiate what you want to attract.
- Believe that you deserve supportive relationships.
- Know that we attract to ourselves what we most need to learn.
- Look for people who are your positive mirrors, they will be good friends.
- Love yourself and you will attract loving relationships.
- Develop strong boundaries.
- Let go of old hurts and move on.

13

Improving Your Health and Fitness Levels

> *'Take a moment — or a lifetime —*
> *to appreciate your body.'*
>
> DAN MILLMAN

Where are you standing on the health and fitness spectrum? If you are struggling with ill health or just want to increase your levels of fitness, the message is the same: you can take charge of your own body. This message sometimes feels uplifting (yes, I will start to exercise regularly) and sometimes feels like a burden (oh, I just can't be bothered to make the effort). Our culture has encouraged us to rely on outside authorities to monitor our health and to 'sort us out' when we are not feeling well, but, whilst professional help can be vitally important, let us never forget that ultimately we are all responsible for our own health and fitness.

So, whether you want to lose weight, tone your muscles, increase your energy levels, let go of stress or improve your overall health, you can do it!

The words 'to heal' literally mean 'to make whole', and this means balancing our spiritual, mental, emotional and physical energies so that we feel healthy and 'at ease'. If there is a block in our energy circuit we are no longer balanced; our energy stops flowing freely and we feel out of sorts with ourselves (not at ease) and eventually can become dis-eased in some way. We have all had experiences where we have made ourselves feel ill because of an emotional reaction. Perhaps you have been 'sick with worry' or had a headache or illness which was brought on by stress. Obviously, our life experiences can contribute towards our state of health: our physical bodies are a part of our mind, spirit and emotions; everything is connected!

Healing Yourself

Our degree of health and fitness can be increased by a two-fold approach. We need to look inside ourselves to evaluate our lifestyles, beliefs, patterns and emotions, and we also need to look out into the world to increase our knowledge of available treatments, approaches, guidance, groups, classes, or whatever support we need.

Let's take the health issue first. If you want to improve your health and decrease the risk of long-term illness be prepared to look inside and outside yourself for guidance. However serious or chronic your illness, and whatever psychological problems confront you, always remember that *you are in charge of your own healing and you can help yourself.*

Your body is a reflection of your inner states so you need to look at your mental and emotional patterns. What are these patterns creating for you on the physical level? Are your beliefs positive and nurturing or are they negative and depressing? Can you let go of your emotions or are they sitting inside you attracting more anger, resentment and stress? Check that you really do want good health. I know this sounds ridiculous – who could imagine wanting to be unwell? However, at a very deep level it's sometimes possible for us to find 'something in it' for us to remain ill. For example, an illness might be a way to avoid certain responsibilities which feel burdensome. Or maybe not being well creates a way to get out of a situation where we were too afraid to assert ourselves (being ill can be used as a way to say 'no'). Perhaps we are ill so that we can give ourselves a deserved rest. Often home and work commitments mean that we push ourselves beyond endurable physical limits and our bodies justifiably rebel and make us stop. Illness brings attention (of a sort) and if we are feeling unloved it can be a way to feel cared for.

Listening to Your Body

Recognize that whenever you are feeling ill your body is trying to tell you something. Slow down, look inside and listen to its messages.

Check your lifestyle and nutrition -- are they supporting good health?

Do you like your job or is it winding you up?

Are your relationships loving and supportive or difficult and stress inducing?

Are your unexpressed emotions giving you an upset stomach?

Is that heavy feeling of responsibility making your neck and shoulders stiff?

Is that sense of never being quite 'good enough' giving you a headache?

Look beyond the symptoms to the whole picture of your life. Do you need to change things to reduce tension and stress? If you do, those pills and potions will never work; there are deeper issues to resolve.

And when you start your quest for diagnosis and treatment, really explore everything that's on offer. Take the prescribed medicine but also investigate complementary alternative and non-invasive approaches. It's easy to obtain lists of qualified alternative practitioners and there are plenty of good books available that can help you. Seek out information; check the Internet, where you will find support groups for almost every condition imaginable! Get in touch with others who can help you and keep an upbeat frame of mind. I know that it isn't very easy to be pioneering and assertive when you are in pain or feeling ill, but being able to take control of some aspect of your condition will always bring you new energy and strength of will.

A very dear friend of mine had a heart attack just over a year ago and has been on a seemingly eternal waiting list for triple bypass surgery. She spent the year in an agony of not knowing and fear. Eventually it got so bad that she decided she would have to fight for herself or risk the consequences. She became more assertive than I have ever seen her, constantly chasing MPs, consultants, doctors and absolutely anyone who could help her. She pestered the medical profession until they gave in and suddenly found a bed for her. My friend was fighting for her life and this gave her massive motivation. Let the desire to be well be your motivation to understand your illness and to discover the treatment that you feel is right for you.

Fit for Life

And now let's look at your own specific fitness needs. Do you want to increase your endurance and stamina so that you have more energy? Would you like to lose weight, tone your muscles and improve your body image? Or maybe you want to increase your mental well being by reducing your stress and anxiety levels. Exercise and wise nutrition together with relaxation techniques can fulfil all of these needs.

Does the very thought of exercise propel you towards the sofa? Sitting around all day can be very tiring whilst even moderate activity is actually an energizing experience. As the blood starts pumping faster through your body you use up calories, tone your muscles, increase your feelgood endorphin and oxygen levels and release stress hormones into your bloodstream; plenty of reasons to get up off that sofa! But you know all this already; the fact that exercise is 'good' for us is not enough to send us out for a jog, off to the gym, to the pool, or even out for a walk. We like our prizes instantly and the start of a fitness regime (however modest) will stretch us as we push that body to new limits. The rewards do come quite quickly, however. Many studies have shown that there is a direct relationship between exercise and a positive mood (and we all know what positivity can do!).

We are often put off exercise because we make unrealistic plans for ourselves. If you want a beautifully toned and sculpted body you will have to put in the time, but you don't have to spend hours in the gym to become fit and less stressed. If you start your fitness regime in a small way (for example, walking to work instead of taking the bus) you will find that your modest achievements will develop your inclination to create new fitness goals.

I don't know if we really are what we eat, but good nutrition must be a part of any fitness plan. A diet of junk food and the lack of a good intake of water will make you feel too lethargic to even make a cup of tea when the adverts come on! I don't need to talk to you about nutrition, we are surrounded with good advice. Get a grip on what you eat, remember it's the fuel for your body and if you give it junk then it won't function properly.

Include some relaxation time in your plan. Tune out from your problems and turn off the television sometimes. Use creative visualization to see yourself feeling fit and healthy and to relax your mind, body, spirit and emotions.

YOUR PERSONAL ACTION PLAN FOR IMPROVING YOUR HEALTH AND FITNESS LEVELS

Again we must go back to your Life Zone Assessment which begins on page 77. Check the answers that you originally gave and then assess where you stand now.

Reassessment of Health and Fitness Life Zone

My present satisfaction level is . . . .

I am happy/unhappy with this score . . . .

I would describe my health and fitness levels as . . . .

When I think about my levels of health and fitness I feel . . . . . .

I believe that being fit and healthy is . . . .

My hopes and fears for my state of fitness and health are . . . . .

. . . .

Before we can bring changes, new motivation and energy into any area of our lives, we always need to look at how and why we created the old realities. What energy patterns have been holding us back? Let's look at some of the thought, feeling and behaviour patterns which have come together to help you to create your present attitudes towards your health and fitness.

Your Attitudes to Health and Illness

Our guiding beliefs in adulthood were largely formed in our early childhood, and so we need to look back in time to see what we have 'learned to be true' about being well and being sick. The following questions might really take some thinking about. If they do, give yourself time to consider them, you might even have to wait for a day or two for the answers to come. If it's possible, it might be useful to talk to your parents about what happened when you were ill as a child.

1 Go back to your childhood and see what you can remember about your childhood illnesses. Dig deep and write down any thoughts, feelings, memories, sensations, fears, and anything else that comes to you.

. . . .

2 How did your parents react to your illnesses? For example, were they fearful, irritated, sympathetic, loving, cold, distant, supportive ...?

. . . .

3 What sort of messages did you receive from your parents about being ill? (Your answers to the previous question might help here.)

. . . .

4 Was there anything that you enjoyed about being ill as a child (attention, hot water bottles, special food ...)?

. . . .

5 Do you think that any of your childhood beliefs about illness are affecting your health today?

. . . .

6 In what ways have you affected your state of health? (Remember all the positive ways you look after yourself; don't just list all the things you feel guilty about.)

. . . .

7 If you are not as healthy as you would like to be, what would you like to change?

. . . .

Review your answers to these questions and see if you can tease out any negative emotional, thought or behaviour patterns that might be helping to create a less than healthy you. Whatever the state of your health, whether you are suffering with difficult mental or physical problems, feeling very ill, or experiencing occasional pain and discomfort, you can always influence the course of your healing.

Your Attitudes to Fitness

We all know that exercise is good for our physical and mental health and that it will improve the way we look. Given all these positives you would imagine that we would all be out there pounding the pavements, swimming lengths, lifting weights, attending aerobics classes ... but no, we strongly resist the call of the exercise drum, and just turn up the volume on the TV instead. The truth is that a good keep-fit regime requires a commitment of time, energy and motivation and it's easy to believe that we haven't any of these to spare. Do you recognize any of the following excuses?

11 ineffective excuses to stop you exercising

1 I haven't got the time.

2 I'm too tired to be bothered.

3 I can't afford to join a gym.

4 I'm basically a lazy person.

5 I've never been a sporty type and I'm completely unco-ordinated.

6 I've been exercising for three weeks and nothing is happening.

7 I find exercising so boring.

8 I'm too fat to wear Lycra.

9 I'm afraid to go to a gym; I won't know what to do and
   I'm embarrassed by my flab.

10 My arm hurts, my head aches, etc.

11 I can't stick at anything and so I know I'd just give up
   too soon.

If you are using any of these excuses it's time to admit that none
of them is valid. Why is it that, at the first mention of exercise,
we are imagining that we have to run marathons, lift huge
weights, swim fifty lengths? No wonder it all seems too much
effort. Keeping fit does not require that you become a world-class
athlete. Nor does it mean that you need a perfect Lycra-clad body
before you can straddle an exercise bike. You don't even have to
go near a gym when a good brisk daily walk will work wonders
(so that injury excuse may prove ineffective, too!). Or how about
taking up salsa dancing? Face your negative attitudes here and
recognize how they are limiting you. Exercise can be great fun;
why not allow yourself the pleasure of a fit and healthy body?

Setting New Goals

Get your goals down on paper, where they seem so much more
real. Decide what you want to achieve in both the health and
fitness areas of your life.

Health goals

Don't expect to conquer your health problems overnight. On the
other hand, do expect to gain some control over your healing.
Carefully review your Attitudes to Health and Illness answers.
What are the underlying patterns that need to be overcome?
What changes would you like to see in your health? Set short
term and long term goals and be prepared to take one step at a
time on the path to recovery. Here are some examples of possible
goals.

Short term

To keep positive even if I feel unwell.

To look at my beliefs surrounding health and illness to see whether they are contributing to my ill health.

To gain as much information as I can about complementary alternative approaches.

Long term

To regain control in my life.

To return to work.

To start a keep-fit plan when I feel better.

To learn to love and value myself, just the way I am.

To appreciate and enjoy my good health.

Don't ever give your power away, however ill you feel. You are the expert at knowing yourself. Keep in touch with your feelings and choose to take control of your own body. Set some specific goals and then work towards them.

Fitness goals

Keep your goals positive or you might find your resolve slipping. For example, if my goals are to lose weight and to stop eating junk food, I will immediately create a headlong conflict with my own willpower. These goals smack of deprivation and I will be severely tempted to break my resolve even before I have begun! So, a good tip here is to always give our goals a positive focus (everything to gain and nothing to lose). If I replace, 'lose weight' with 'take some exercise and tone up', then I am looking at a positive outcome and I have more chance of achieving my goal. Similarly, if I replace, 'stop eating junk food' with 'eat a more healthy diet and find out more about good nutrition', I can get to grips with my new project rather than focus on all the things I shouldn't be eating.

Write down your own short and long term fitness goals. Here are a few examples.

Short term

To drink at least a litre of water a day.

To ride my bike to work.

To eat more fruit and vegetables.

To make sure I get at least twenty minutes a day in the fresh air.

To walk around the block in my lunch hour.

Long term

To learn more about good nutrition and buy some new cookery books.

To improve my body image by increasing my levels of exercise.

To take up a new interest which will help me to get physically fit (dancing, golf, jogging, swimming, a martial art, yoga ...).

Let your goals reflect what you want to happen and take everything one step at a time. Do one thing every day towards improving your fitness levels and you will be gratified by the eventual results.

Realizing Your Health Goals

You know that taking control of your health and fitness issues depends upon your level of motivation. From a holistic perspective this will mean making positive changes at all levels of your being: mental, spiritual, emotional and physical. Let's look at how you can achieve your health goals.

Achieving your health goals

Reflect upon all your answers to the exercises which refer to your health. Look carefully at your hopes and fears; your beliefs and emotions surrounding health and illness, and take particular notice of your childhood memories. Can you bring together any strands of thoughts and feelings which could be stopping you creating good health?

Your mental energy

Look at your goals. What do you want to achieve? Now, consider any of your thoughts, beliefs and ideas which might stop you. Make a list in your journal.

> The thoughts, beliefs and ideas that might stop me realizing my
> health goals are . . . .
>
> . . . .

If one of my goals is 'to keep positive even if I feel unwell' and one of my beliefs is 'I only get attention when others feel sorry for me', then my need for attention might outweigh my desire to be more upbeat. Can you see how important it is to recognize and understand the unconscious beliefs that are running our lives (and our health)? If you are running with any negative patterns which support illness rather than health then these must be changed. Please don't make yourself 'wrong' in any way, we all have negative patterns to overcome. If you have unearthed any negative beliefs don't beat yourself up about it (this approach would make you feel even worse). Recognize any negative beliefs and then let them go. You do this, not by going over and over the past, but by focusing on the power of the moment. You can change your life in an instant; it is only a decision away. Decide to surround yourself with healing consciousness and feel your energy respond. Replace limiting thoughts and ideas by speaking aloud (or singing, writing, shouting ...) your positive affirmations for health. Use the list below if you wish and also create some healing affirmations of your own.

Positive affirmations for health

I deserve vibrant health
I can heal myself
It is safe to be well
I create harmony and balance within my body
I am ready to be well, now
I trust my inner messages

I love my body
The universal life force flows easily through me
I love and value myself

Decide right now to:
love yourself,
forgive yourself,
trust your intuition,
release all blame,
express your needs,
take responsibility for your health.

You are a unique, amazing and valuable person and you deserve to be healthy!

Your spiritual energy

Use the process of creative visualization to affirm your health goals. Go into a relaxed state and experience the realization of your goals. See yourself radiating energy, health and well being. Take each of your positive affirmations for health and visualize their reality. How do you look? How do you feel? Replace those old negative pictures with your new and vibrant images.

Your emotional energy

Intention and desire are the driving forces behind the achievement of your goals. If you are still lacking the commitment to improve your health issues, you need to look at your emotional energy. Review all your answers in this action plan and then consider your feelings in relation to your responses. Your emotional energy will block your motivation if you are holding on to feelings which need to be expressed. Is there something you need to say? Is there someone you need to say it to? Is there anything that you have found hard to face or have been unable to admit to yourself? Answer these questions now in your journal and, as you clear out your emotional debris, you will feel your motivation increase.

Your physical energy

And now for some action! You are not a victim of circumstances, you can always take charge of your life. Ask for what you want; express your needs and seek out any knowledge and information which is related to your health problem. Don't be intimidated by medical jargon; ask the questions you need to ask; seek out a second opinion (and more) if you are not satisfied with a diagnosis. Be proactive instead of reactive and you will immediately begin to feel better about yourself.

Realizing Your Fitness Goals

Achieving your fitness goals

Are you still making any of the 11 ineffective excuses? Our self-motivation (or lack of it) becomes very visible when we enter the fitness arena. The only way to start that body really moving is to focus entirely on positive gains. Remind yourself how good you will feel after exercising and forget about the comfort of the sofa (you can sit on it when you get back!). Which of those excuses are you still hanging on to? Or maybe you have created some of your own. Write down all your 'good' reasons for not exercising.

I cannot exercise in any way because . . . .

. . . .

Your mental energy

Go back to your fitness goals and then back to your excuses. If your goal is to start some modest exercise by cycling to work, but one of your excuses (to yourself) is that you are 'basically a lazy person', then this mental conflict will ensure that you will never get on your bike. So many people believe that they are lazy and yet human energy is naturally inquisitive, changing, moving and achieving. Laziness is just a state of mind, which we use as an excuse when we are feeling challenged. Sitting indoors, watching TV, might seem to be the most non-threatening activity on the planet, but of course it is most threatening to our physical and mental well being. Take your excuses, one at a time, and look for the negative pattern inherent in each one. Then create a positive affirmation which contradicts your excuse. For example:

My excuse	My new positive affirmation
I haven't got the time	I am good at organizing my time
I'm too tired	Exercise makes me more energetic
Exercise is so boring	I love stretching my body and feeling it really doing some work
I'm too fat to wear Lycra	I am sticking to my weight loss and exercise plan and in ... (fill in your own time here) I will be able to wear Lycra
My arm hurts	Walking is good all-round exercise

Make your goals attractive. Specify time limits in which to achieve your goals. Applaud yourself whenever you reach a goal. Once you start a fitness plan and see and feel the benefits (which happens quite soon) you will become fired with enthusiasm. I see two sorts of people at the gym: reluctant newcomers who wearily and warily climb on to the equipment and fitness enthusiasts who love to exercise. After about two months, the newcomers who stuck it out have joined the ranks of enthusiasts. A daily short walk can start to become something you can't do without. A bike ride can brighten your day. Just get to the bottom of your excuses and begin!

Your spiritual energy

Change those inner pictures of Lycra-clad embarrassment, aching limbs, tiredness, lethargy and boredom. Visualize the newly toned and supple you. See and feel yourself enjoying your chosen exercises: swimming, walking, cycling, yoga, weights ... Let go of any images that limit you. Make the new pictures positively vibrant and energetic because you will become the person that you are visualizing.

Your emotional energy

Because your emotional energy can block your motivation, check any feelings which might be holding you back. Look your fears in the face and then step beyond them. New activities always involve risk-taking. Face your embarrassment and shyness and just get going; you have everything to gain and nothing to lose (except maybe some excess weight).

Your physical energy

Here are some strategies to kick-start your physical energy.

Plan tomorrow's exercise today. Decide what you are going to do and how long it will take.

Be realistic. Fitness doesn't come overnight, but the first step towards it does. Stick to your plan and the results will come.

Be creative. A few hours in the garden is a brilliant way to work your body. Always use the stairs. Welcome every exercise opportunity: carrying the shopping, having sex, washing the floor and putting out the rubbish are all activities which will increase your fitness levels. Enjoy using your body!

Take some risks. As your fitness levels increase why not introduce a new activity to challenge you and to keep you interested?

For New Health and Fitness Levels

- Always remember that ultimately you are in charge of your own body.

- Look beyond your symptoms to the whole picture of your life.

- Seek out any information and support that you need.

- Work towards realistic goals and be nice to yourself every step of the way.

- Listen to the messages your body sends; what is it trying to tell you?

- Visualize your new, improved levels of health and fitness and then take whatever action you need to achieve them.

- Love your body and it will respond magnificently.

- You can do it!

14

Increasing Your Wealth

*'And you know I really do believe in the fact that
you manifest what you think in this world.'*

JIM CARREY

Top funny-man Jim Carrey is a self-confessed positive thinker.
Before he became a Hollywood player, in the days when he was
a struggling comedian, he wrote himself a cheque for $7 million.
You might wonder why he did this, but it was in fact a fine
demonstration of his knowledge of the 4 Principles of Creativity.
He says that it was his way of visualizing, seeing himself saying
'That puts me in with the top guys.' He says that was his dream
and that *he still dreams about it*. Jim Carrey *passionately
believed* that he would succeed, he *expected* to see cheques
paying him millions of dollars, and still maintains his dream (he
actually earned about $20 million from his latest movie). Now I
know that we are not all movie stars with the potential to earn
bucketloads of cash, but we can all use our understanding of the
creative laws to increase our wealth and prosperity.

When Is Enough Enough?

Money, like sex, is always a potentially volatile issue. I once
heard someone say that she thought that money was like sex, in
the sense that when you don't have enough of it you keep
thinking about it, and when you do have enough of it you have
the energy to think about other things!

Well, how much money is 'enough'? What can money bring us? Can we ever have sufficient? Thinking about money really stirs up our emotions: we worry (about not having enough); we want more (we can never have enough); we exchange our labour for it (are we being paid fairly?); we worship it (and lose sight of our true purpose in life); we love it, save it, spend it and squander it and some people have even killed for it! So don't be surprised if your relationship with money is a complex one. And just like all your other relationships, this one is also a reflection of where you are at in your life. We will see that a lack of money merely mirrors our own negative patterning.

The Quest for Security

Whilst writing this chapter I did some informal research on the ways that various friends, colleagues and acquaintances relate to the money issue. It seems that everyone can talk for a long time about the ins and outs of their financial lives! But once all the worries, complaints, spending and saving habits have been mentioned, everyone said that the most important thing that money can bring is security.

Financial security means that you will never, ever again have to worry about not having enough money because you have amassed enough for your lifetime. How realistic is this for most of us? The pursuit of complete financial security is a never-ending quest which will not give us the security that we seek. Security cannot come from money because *money is only a symbol of our creative energy*. Simply put, this means that, you use your energy to create money and then trade that money to someone else in exchange for whatever their energy has created. Because we know that there is an infinite supply of universal creative energy and that we have unlimited access to this energy (and indeed are a part of this abundant supply), our potential to attract money must also be limitless. Our security can only lie in the awareness of the abundant nature of the universe: if there is always plenty of everything to go round, why would we ever feel insecure?

Security is an inner state which we can only ever achieve by recognizing such truths as: the universe and all its occupants are intimately connected; the world is a safe place; we all deserve the best in life; human beings are always doing the best they can; the universe supports us at all times; we each create our own reality, and we can transform our lives (and the planet) by the powers of positive thought and positive action. When we are moved by love instead of fear we don't need wads of cash to make us feel secure. However, when we believe in an abundant, giving and supportive universe we do actually start to bring more money into our lives!

Imagine this. There are two people. One is rich in money but insecure about how to keep it (is afraid of being robbed and/or feels guilty about his wealth). The other has less money but knows how to enjoy what he has and how to make the best of his life. Who is the more wealthy in the resources of life? Who feels more prosperous? *Our prosperity consciousness does not depend on our wealth; actually, our wealth depends upon our prosperity consciousness.* Feel rich in the good things of life and they will be attracted to you.

Abundance and Prosperity

When you feel prosperous you are full of life and well being and you radiate a sense of generosity, trust, open-heartedness and abundance. Because prosperity issues are always about the quality of our individual lives, an increase in prosperity will mean different things to each of us. We can have lots of money and still not feel affluent because prosperity is a feeling of fulfilment, satisfaction and self-esteem, and money cannot buy any of these things. Think about what prosperity means to you. Are you rich in health, spirituality, success, friendships, family, self-awareness, love? If you feel a deficiency in any area of your life it is always easy to blame it on money (or rather, the lack of money). As you have worked through this book you will now know for sure that money cannot buy you the qualities that you desire (although it can buy you a nice dress or a nice car!). Positive life changes depend upon a positive outlook. A negative, fear-based lifestyle will keep us in scarcity consciousness for a lifetime and a sense of lack will pervade all our life zones, including the money zone. Surround yourself with abundance awareness and every aspect of your life will magically improve and you will be able to buy that dress or that car!

Whenever you feel impoverished, there is never enough of what you want. It could be attention, love, money, happiness, success, confidence, commitment, tender loving care, respect ... add your own 'lacks' to this list. As soon as you sense a feeling of scarcity within you, you can change this energy. Think of the 4 Principles of Creativity: scarcity begets scarcity as fear closes down our creativity, and abundance attracts even more of the same. You attract whatever you are radiating and your thoughts are like magnets (so watch the way they are going). Change your 'poor' energy for 'rich' energy by making affirmations of prosperity (we will look at how to do this in the action plan).

Magnetizing Money

But maybe having more money *would* increase your prosperity. If you are always worrying about your lack of finances you will attract further lack. If you keep sending out negative messages of money deprivation and poverty, your unconscious will dutifully manifest these things in your life (so you will just keep getting even more of the same, which actually means getting less and less money).

We know that thoughts are things and that they fly out into the world like magnets which attract their duplicates in material form. What are your thoughts magnetizing? Our deep beliefs about money, and about what we deserve, are thought magnets which can make or break us financially. For example, if you believe that money is in some way unclean, then it's unlikely that you will ever be able to let it flow easily into your life (you would always be too afraid of its bad influence). And if your deservabilty levels are low (you believe that you are not good enough to deserve much, or even anything) then you will certainly never be able to attract money. Again we find that our beliefs are the decisive factors in our lives. People who love money and have an easy relationship with it (one not fraught with worry and anguish) find it easy to draw riches into their lives. So, instead of worrying about money (Will it last? Will there be enough? Will I be able to pay the bills?) take a more creative approach. Ask yourself how you can create more money. Forget about the fearful, 'What will I do?' and introduce the empowering, 'What can I do?' Yes, you are at the creative centre of your life. Create!

Looking at Your Money Habits

One powerful and practical way to create money is to take a long, cool look at our spending and saving habits. Some people are natural savers and not surprisingly these types have some money! Natural savers are really good at not buying everything they fancy; they can go into a fabulous clothes store with money and/or credit cards and can walk out without buying a *single thing*. Sadly, I am not one of these types and it's only fairly recently that I realized that I couldn't have any savings unless I had saved them! Ah well, in the same way that some people can stop eating when they are full, others can window shop (and this is enough!). The rest of us might find such behaviour impossible (although highly commendable). The strong-willed amongst you will inevitably have good financial habits; this section is for the rest of us.

If you admit to loving retail therapy then check out the following.

- We can 'fake it 'til we make it' in many areas of our lives but not in this one. If we act confident we will start to feel it; if we act calmly we will feel more peaceful; if we act assertively we will start to feel in control. But, if we act as if we have more money than we have, and actually go out and spend it, we will be in big trouble. If you are a natural spender you will need to change your habits (take heart, there are many of us).

- Think before you spend. Do you really have to buy that divine pair of pink suede boots which cost a week's salary. How many hours of your energy will you be exchanging for them? Ask yourself, 'Are they really worth it?' Walk away if you have one shred of doubt. Natural savers never squander money, they have too much respect for it.

- Start a money diary in your journal. I know this sounds terrifying but it really is empowering. For a week, write down everything you spend; coffees, meals, all items of food shopping, drinks in the pub, petrol, cream cakes at lunchtime ... (that weekly cake habit might cost you more than a night out at the movies). Think of this task as one which will help you to reallocate your income. It's amazing how we can continually spend large quantities of small amounts (how many new types of conditioner do I really need to try in one week?) and deny ourselves something big. One friend actually gave up cigarettes after doing this financial inventory, saved the money for a year and went to Thailand for a holiday. So you see this new habit could lead to great things! Checking expenditure against income contravenes the impulsive nature of all natural spenders, we hate financial constraints and the limitations of orderly and controlled expenditure. Look, just do it for a week to see where your money is dribbling away. When you take up your old impulsive ways again in a week at least you will know why you never have any cash!

- Save money if you want to have any savings. This came as such a revelation to me. If you put some money away regularly it has a fantastic effect. You are in effect saying, 'I have more than enough'. This belief is a great money magnet.

- Give with gratitude and bless the outward going and the inward coming money. Be happy that you can pay what you owe, and give with love. Be generous with others and you will be amazed at what happens. Gratitude, love and appreciation open the doors to abundance (and more of everything). Love money for the creative power that it represents and all that you give will be returned many times over.

YOUR PERSONAL ACTION PLAN FOR INCREASING YOUR WEALTH

Talking about the secret of wealth in his book *Bring out the Magic in Your Mind*, stage magician Al Koran said, 'Some people say "when my ship comes in". Good gracious, it has been in the harbour for years waiting to be unloaded, and you didn't know it!' This is a great image isn't it? Your ship is in, full of all the good things you could wish for, just get down to that harbour and start unloading.

Your beliefs and outlook will determine your capacity to attract abundance and wealth, and this action plan will help you to create a new upbeat approach towards your finances. Think rich and you will attract riches, think poor and stay poor.

Look back to your Life Zone Assessment for money and then make your reassessment. In what ways, if any, has your attitude towards money changed?

Reassessment of Money Zone

My present satisfaction level is ....

I am happy/unhappy with this score ....

I would describe my money situation as ....

When I think about money I feel ....

I believe that money is ....

My hopes and fears about money are ....

Reflect on your answers in the light of what you have read earlier in this chapter. Can you recognize any thoughts, feelings and behaviours which could be damming your flow of riches? Where are you creating scarcity, lack and deprivation in your life? Why not decide to create prosperity instead?

Your Attitudes to Money

Let's examine some of your underlying thoughts, feelings and actions in relation to money. Answer these questions in your journal.

1 What is your biggest worry in connection with money?

2 What are (or were) your parents' beliefs about money?

3 How were financial matters dealt with by your family when you were growing up?

4 How do you deal with money matters now?

5 Would you describe yourself as a saver, a spender or somewhere in the middle?

6 How does your answer to the last question affect your cash flow?

7 How do you feel when you are spending money? Anxious, exhilarated, angry, empty, full, buoyant, depressed, anything else?

8 Would you like to change the ways that you deal with money? What would you like to be different?

9 What is your wildest fantasy in connection with money?

10 If you won a million how do you think it would change your life?

It's not hard to see how we create our patterns around money. If your parents suffered from a lack of money and were constantly worried about how the next bill would be paid, then this will have its effect on you in some way. If either of your parents was a spendthrift you might also be, or perhaps you are rebelling against this behaviour and like to hoard money. Whatever you discover about your limiting habits and emotions around money, let it work for you. Use this information to change your prosperity levels. It's always easy to change our patterns once we decide to do so. How wonderful would it be to feel relaxed and happy about your financial issues? How amazing would it feel to be able to pay your bills happily? This is all possible for you. Forgive your parents for teaching you ways that might have limited rather than expanded your financial potential. Put yourself in their shoes: how would you have acted, given their own background and circumstances? Let go of all self-blame (criticism always encourages limitation) and embrace your new expansive consciousness. Check your beliefs and expectations about money; do they encourage abundance and prosperity or are they based on scarcity and lack?

Your beliefs about money

Look at the following statements.

- Money doesn't grow on trees.

- I am poor but honest.

- Having no money helps me stay focused on my spiritual path.

- I would only feel guilty about it if I had money.

- Money is dirty.

- Really creative types never get rich.

- People with money exploit those without.

- If I got rich I wouldn't know who my friends were.

- You only get money by working hard all the time.

- My folks were poor and I'm just the same.

- I'm not educated enough to make money.

- If I had lots of money it might ruin my life.

If you believe any of these things then you will be surrounded with poverty energy and this is what you will attract. The truth is that money is not intrinsically bad; how can it be when it is only a symbol of our creative energy? Don't blame money for the ways that people can behave. It is just as possible to be dishonest and poor as it is to be rich and generous. Trust yourself to know how to behave towards people whatever your financial circumstances and don't be afraid to choose beliefs that will help you to attract money into your life.

Setting New Goals

As we become more conscious of our limiting patterns and we look closely at our spending/squandering/saving habits, it becomes feasible to imagine increasing our wealth. Goals that might have seemed far-fetched or impossible before now start to feel achievable. Set down on paper some short-term goals (achievable in three months and under) and long-term goals. Go one step at a time, or you will try to do too much at once and won't be able to achieve your goal. For example, saving for a holiday is a long-term goal, you can't expect to raise the money in less than three months. But you can make various short-term goals which work towards long-term achievements. Make sure that your short-term goals don't make you feel deprived or you might blow all your good intentions on a wild spree.

Set some realistic goals and you will definitely reap financial benefits. A few examples follow.

Short term

To assess my income/expenditure details.

To work to a monthly budget.

To save a small amount each month so that I can reward myself when I achieve my goals.

To start asking myself, 'Do I really need this?' before I buy something.

To make lists of essential items before I go shopping and to stick to the lists.

To start working on increasing my prosperity consciousness.

To accept that I don't have to keep up with anyone else's
spending habits.

Long term

To take some financial advice.

To increase my earnings.

To save for a holiday.

To start a pension plan/savings fund.

To always know where I stand financially so that I never
spend beyond my means.

To become more relaxed about money issues.

To bring abundance and prosperity into all parts of my life.

Realizing Your Goals

Achieving your financial goals will always require a shift in consciousness; *out of* scarcity and deprivation and *into* prosperity
and abundance. Whenever you start to feel your energy drifting
down into feelings of poverty and lack, step out into prosperity
consciousness by creating positive affirmations of abundance.
Look at the following list and choose any that you feel are meaningful to you. Then create some of your own, by taking any of
your scarcity beliefs and turning them right around to produce
contradictory prosperity beliefs. For example, if you discover
that deep down you believe that *we are all in competition with
each other*, you could create the new belief that *we are all here
to work together*. Let your new positive beliefs create your new
prosperous reality, by repeating these affirmations to yourself.
Steep yourself in prosperity consciousness and your whole world
will take on new colour, meaning and purpose.

Affirmations of abundance

The universe always supports me.

I am ready to enjoy my life.

Whatever I give is always returned many times over.

Life is a celebration.

The abundance of the universe is mine.

We are here to take care of each other.

There is nothing to fear.

Infinite riches flow freely into my life.

I love money.

Nature has abundant resources, there is plenty of everything to go round.

I am rich, healthy and happy.

Achieving your money goals

Now look carefully at your goals. What beliefs and attitudes are holding you back? What do you need to change to allow yourself access to the infinite flow of universal abundance? If you only take a teaspoon to the ocean, you will only be able to take away one teaspoon of water. There is an infinite ocean of resources available and you can have all that you want: everyone can have all that they want! Make sure that the receptacle you bring (your consciousness) does not limit the amount that you can have. Check out any limiting thought, feeling and behaviour patterns.

Your mental energy

Whenever you feel ready to change your money consciousness, you can use the following five steps which will cleverly unearth and change the sources of your limiting poverty patterns. The *belief* behind your limitation enables you to create a new contradictory affirmation of abundance which then leads you into positive change.

1 Take any limiting action or feeling connected with money.

2 Discover the *belief* behind this limitation.

3 Make affirmations of abundance to lift your energy into prosperity consciousness.

4 Ask yourself why you are hanging on to old limitations.

5 Declare that you are ready to change.

Here is an example.

1 Action: I am tight with money; I can only ever buy things that are reduced in price.

2 Belief: My parents were poor and so am I.

3 Affirmation: I attract money and I deserve financial success.

4 Reason for belief: I have been running with this belief because if I'm poor others won't feel threatened by me and so they will like me (I will stay one of the gang).

5 Declaration: I am ready to change now!

You can easily discover the underlying scarcity beliefs behind any limiting actions and feelings. Use this five-step approach when you really feel ready to commit to changing your money consciousness. You will be astonished by how easy it is to begin to feel rich and wealthy; just allow prosperity into your life and appreciate the changes it brings.

Your spiritual energy

Whatever you have been visualizing is coming true for you right now. Thoughts are magnets and so are the images that you are carrying. What financial realities have you been visualizing? Use your imagination to expand your boundaries. Think of your goals and visualize your new expansive outcomes. Ignore thoughts such as, 'that's impossible', or 'it will never work'; look where such thoughts have got you. Push back all the boundaries and visualize more than enough of everything in your life. Take a few minutes out every day to go into a relaxed state and to consciously manifest your heart's desire. Don't worry, you can have more than you need without someone else going short: there is more than enough of everything to go round. Everyone can live in abundance.

Your emotional energy

Money is such an emotive issue that I know you will have discovered many feelings which you will need to express or work through in some other way. Don't get bogged down by strong emotions because they will undermine the clarity of your intentions. Recognize the strength of your feelings and then you must move beyond them, because they will be attached to your limiting beliefs. As you step out of scarcity and into prosperity you leave behind any restricting beliefs and feelings; let go and move forward into the life you deserve.

Your physical energy

Affirmations of abundance and visualizations of achieving your goals are very powerful inner tools. But they must be accompanied by action in the outer world if you want to create a prosperous lifestyle. You know the money habits that you need to change. You know that you cannot have a savings account if you just stay at home visualizing it. Match your inner awareness with appropriate action and your life will change before your very eyes. If compulsive spending is your problem then you must find a way to stop. If your money is dribbling away into nothingness then make that financial inventory and see exactly where it is all going. Change your money habits into good ones that are empowering and enriching!

For New and Increased Wealth

- Get down to the harbour and start unloading your ship.

- Magnetize money into your life.

- Create good money habits.

- Give with gratitude and bless the money that passes through your hands.

- Love money and it will love you back.

- Forgive and let go of old hurts, they keep you in limitation and scarcity.

- Embrace the abundance of the universe.

- Remember that we are all connected.

- Consciously manifest your heart's desire.

- Think prosperous and you will be prosperous.

- Always be generous.

15

Discovering Your Life's Work

'Everybody is an artist, everybody is creative, everybody can do work they love.'

MIKE PEGG

A number of years ago my own career path led me to working with young adults who were unemployed, and also with young people who were about to leave school and were struggling with very low levels of motivation. These jobs were very demanding and stretched my personal resources to the limit, but they were also highly rewarding and exhilarating. What I saw in those training rooms and classrooms absolutely convinced me of the truth that we can, and do, create our own reality.

When Kahlil Gibran wrote that 'Work is love made visible', he touched upon our need to lead a usefully creative life. If young people feel that they are unemployable and have nothing to offer their community they sink to the depths of low self-esteem and either give up completely or become aggressive. As you can imagine, the energy levels of these groups was initially very low and at first I had to do some quite outrageous things to attract the participants' attention! But something amazing always happened. As soon as these youngsters felt that there was hope for them and that they were not the total failures they thought they were, a new positive energy would flow through the group and extraordinary changes occurred.

Whenever anyone learns to value their own unique set of skills and strengths they can recognize that, yes, they really do have a contribution to make. I have many inspiring stories to tell about how some of these deprived youngsters managed to pull themselves up out of their powerlessness and into a creative future. As our self-belief and expectations change we undoubtedly attract new energy and opportunities. And I watched with amazement the way that doors would 'magically' open for these young people once they started to believe in themselves and became focused and ready to move on.

What Do You Most Love About Your Life?

But we don't have to be unemployed to feel undervalued and dissatisfied with work issues. We spend a large chunk of our lives in work, and if we are not happy there, we need to make some changes. You *can* do the work you would love to do; imagine jumping out of bed every Monday morning full of the joys of spring! This is not an impossibility. What do you love to do? What is it that inspires and motivates you? What is important to you? What touches your heart? What brings value to your life? What really gets you going and stirs up your passions? The answers to these questions will give you some important personality clues.

Isn't it amazing that we find this sort of question so unusual? When I ask people what they most love about living, they are usually taken aback, shocked and embarrassed by such an 'in your face' approach. But why is this? When we know what inspires and delights a person we gain an extraordinary insight into their personality. Why isn't this the first question we ask people when we meet them rather than the last thing we would ever dream of asking? Isn't it sad that some people can go through their whole life without knowing what they most love about being alive; perhaps no one ever asked them and so they never thought to ask themselves. If we don't know what excites and energizes us we will never be able to tap into the infinitely creative energy of the universe; we will never realize our full potential. Good reason, therefore, to get to grips with the following questions. Answer them in your journal and be as specific and detailed as you can. Whatever it is that inspires and motivates you will be a pointer towards where your true talents and skills will be found. Don't be shy about your interests and passions. Think about what really gets your creative juices flowing. What are the things that you most love about being alive?

What do I most enjoy doing? List twenty things that give you pleasure. For example, walking on a beach, making biscuits, gardening, riding a bike along country lanes, going out with my family, reading the Sunday papers in bed, swimming, going to the theatre ...

What are my passions? These are the things that really inspire and motivate you; they totally focus your attention and channel your energy. Some examples I've heard include supporting Arsenal, being a vegetarian, playing in the local rugby team, being in a rock band, writing poetry, keeping fit, supporting my family, yoga, organic gardening, model railways. Your passions are anything that will inspire you to jump out of bed in the morning in a hopeful and expectant mood!

What am I good at? List your skills and strengths. This is not just a list of your paper qualifications (although of course it will include them). You will find that you are usually good at what you enjoy. Examples are being sociable, giving great parties, using the computer, playing football, being responsible, getting the best from people, cooking Indian food, time management, being optimistic most of the time. Look carefully at the qualities you need to demonstrate your skills (the person in the example is a good communicator and organizer who is outgoing and has a positive outlook).

Far from having few skills and strengths you will find that you have many, and you can use these abilities and personal qualities to expand your work horizons. As they say in the career counselling business, 'Getting a job is a job in itself'. And the first step is to know your own value in the workplace.

When do I really feel in the flow? When your creative energy is flowing you feel fabulous, energetic, focused, absorbed, playful, light and productive. When are you at your most creative? Are there any ways that you can make your work more creative and enjoyable? Are there new directions you need to take to make your working life a pleasurable and fulfilling experience?

What Is Your Life's Work?

Fascination, motivation, aliveness, energy, focus, commitment and enthusiasm are all qualities which you possess when you are following your true path and fulfilling the unique contribution you came to make. When you are using your special gifts and talents in this way you are doing your life's work, and this may involve a job where you earn money or it may not.

When my children were very small it gave me great satisfaction and purpose to look after them, and this felt like my life's work. When they grew older and more independent I turned back to my own career path because my own needs were different, and so my life's work changed again (it became a combination of mothering and writing). Our paths are always moving and taking us in new directions, and our levels of satisfaction/dissatisfaction provide clues to which routes to take along the way. When we follow our hearts and do what we most love to do we are doing our life's work. Sometimes this might mean keeping the 'day' job until you are well placed to launch your dream career. Sometimes earning a living and supporting your family can feel like an extremely worthwhile and creative experience (even if the job is not so great). If we appreciate our work for the money that it brings this can so alter our attitude that this in itself can prompt changes.

I knew a man who had been unemployed for six years. He had previously been self-employed, running his own business and making a very good living. One day he fell and seriously hurt his back and couldn't work for a long time. He lost his business and claimed sickness benefit and his family scraped by. This man, who had once been a well-motivated self-starter, and an employer, had lost all his confidence and self-esteem since his accident (this is what unemployment does to most people). When I met him in a workshop for the long-term unemployed he was absolutely desperate to find work. He told me that he would be prepared to do almost anything if only he could provide for his family and become independent again. He took a job in a warehouse, clearing up and caretaking, and I never saw a man so thrilled to get a job. He was so delighted and proud to be working again and he just carried that in his aura. I love this story, which brilliantly demonstrates the way that we can create our own reality. This man radiated interest and enthusiasm at work and soon got noticed. He was quickly promoted to general warehouse duties and, two years later, was working in a managerial role. It was easy to see how he had attracted this reality; appreciation can sometimes move mountains.

Ask yourself if there is anything about your present job that you are not appreciating fully. If there is, then see what happens when you change your attitude (you might not have to change your job at all).

Your Mission and Your Mortgage

Someone might become quite clear about what inspires and motivates her (she loves being with people, travelling, new experiences ...) but of course, she also need to pay the bills (and so she works in an office). If the office work funds her travelling and new experiences then maybe it gives her what she needs. On the other hand, if working indoors at a desk is driving her crazy she might need to rethink her mission and mortgage balance.

When we can put our interests and talents to work for us and earn money doing what we love, we have balanced our mission (our life's work at the moment) with our mortgage (the need to earn money). It is a great gift to be able to earn enough money by doing the things that interest you most and, although this might seem impossible for you at the moment, it is always possible to work towards this goal. Ask yourself if there is any way that you can combine the activities you love with earning money. Start to make financial links with your favourite activities and skills and you might be amazed at how soon a hobby or interest can turn into a part-time or even a full-time job.

For example, a friend of mine started making beautiful patchwork cushions as a relaxing pastime and she gave them away as presents. So many people admired her work and asked her to make them cushions but she found it hard to put a realistic price on her labour and at first she undersold herself. Eventually, she put her prices up and turned what had become a part-time money earner into a full-time job, supplying upmarket craft shops. When we are used to giving our services for nothing it can take a big leap to put a fair price on our labour. If you are good at something and other people value your skills why not start to charge for your services? Who knows where it might lead?

Mary, a colleague of mine, described herself as being 'bored to death' by an administrative post in a school. She originally took the job because it was conveniently close to home and it fitted in well with her children's holidays. Mary is a real 'people person', she is so good at making others feel relaxed and she has always had lots of friends. Everyone took their worries to Mary and came away feeling better. A chance remark changed her working life. A friend was sharing a cup of tea (and her miseries) with Mary one day and happened to say, 'Honestly, Mary, you are as good as any counsellor could be.' And this set Mary thinking. She loved listening to people and found their problems fascinating; how wonderful it would be to be able to make a career out of her skills. And so Mary took some career advice and found a suitable course. She took a counselling qualification in the evenings, keeping her day job, and in three years she had good professional credentials. Her first paid work as a counsellor was for a few hours a week in a doctor's surgery, and so she carried on with part-time work at the school to supplement her income. Eventually, she had enough private clients to give up the school job and work full-time as a counsellor.

Don't let the need for any qualifications stand in the way of turning your career dream into a reality. Look for creative ways to overcome your obstacles and keep the day job whilst you develop any skills you might need.

Many people have taken this path before you; it is highly unusual for someone to just 'drop into' their true vocation. It usually takes some time to discover your life's work, and then it takes some more time to make that discovery work for you financially. Be patient, remain focused and keep moving towards your goal; this is the way to success.

You are a skilled and talented person
and you deserve a creative working life.

YOUR PERSONAL ACTION PLAN FOR DISCOVERING YOUR LIFE'S WORK

Whenever we look outside ourselves for the answers to our life questions we are focusing in the wrong place. I know it is tempting to think of the world of work as an external influence over which you have no control; it does seem very much part of the outside world with its own rules and regulations. But remember this: everything is connected, you attract whatever you radiate, you magnetize whatever you think you deserve and so you create your own realities. This is just as true in the work-place as it is in all the other zones. Don't try to work out what to do with your life by looking at the career opportunities and trying to see where you can fit. Rather, look inside yourself and ask, 'What do I want to do? Where do my interests lie? What fascinates me? How can I create my perfect job?' You can take charge of the way that you earn your living; let it be a creative and fulfilling experience.

Go back to your Life Zone Assessment for work (page 79) and make a reassessment. Don't be surprised if you find that your attitudes, beliefs and feelings towards your work have changed.

Reassessment of Work Zone

My present satisfaction level is . . . .

I am happy/unhappy with this score . . . .

I would describe my work situation as . . . .

When I think about work I feel . . . .

I believe that work is . . . .

My hopes and fears about work are . . . .

The strong themes in this book might already be having a profound effect on your life. A positive, creative outlook attracts new vibrant energy and opportunities, and small inner changes have a massive effect in the outside world. For example, any small movement out of scarcity consciousness and into prosperity consciousness will have dramatic repercussions in every area of your life. Your Life Zones don't really stand alone, they have a knock-on effect and a change from 'poor' energy into 'rich' energy would certainly be attracting new possibilities into your work zone.

Do you still feel a sense of limitation around your work issues? Where do you lack the confidence to change? What is holding you back?

Your Attitudes to Work

Answer these questions in your journal to help clarify why you are experiencing any restrictions in the workplace.

1 Do you feel that your work is useful?
(Answer yes or no.)

2 Why do you think it is/isn't useful?

3 What don't you like about your job?

4 How could any of these things be changed?

5 Would you like to alter your career path?

6 What is stopping you?

7 Can you imagine being happy at work? If you can what would be making you happy?

8 Do you think that your beliefs about money are affecting your work choices? If so, how?

9 Would you describe yourself as a person who likes to take responsibility?

Go through your answers very carefully. What sort of person are you? What are your values? Does your work allow you to do what you believe in or are you being compromised?

Sometimes we find ourselves trapped in a lifestyle which doesn't fit us any more. We can become stuck in a job just because it's what we have always done, or it's what our parents wanted us to do, or it was a good idea at the time but now things have changed. To be happy at work means to feel valued, creative and useful and it doesn't necessarily depend on status. I have a friend who was a solicitor in London for twelve years before she decided that downsizing would make her much happier. She moved to the countryside and now works as a fundraiser for a charity. She earns a quarter of her former salary, but she is much happier now.

Of course, you may be unhappy at work because you would like a more responsible job. If this is the case then ask yourself if you need more qualifications. Take careers advice and check out any courses that will give you the confidence and/or the qualifications you need to step up the career ladder.

Imagining your perfect job

Let's bring together all the parts needed to create your perfect job. If this just feels like a dream which could never come true, recall the way our beliefs and visualizations create our realities. If you keep thinking about what is wrong with your job and replaying negative scenarios you will only attract more of the same (we always get more of what we focus upon). It's now time to concentrate on what you want from your job. Fantasize as freely as you wish. Think as big as you can; let there be no limitations. Suspend disbelief and answer these questions as if you are already doing the job. Write the answers in your journal.

1 Describe your working environment. Do you travel to work? If so, how? Are you in a city, a town or in the country?

2 What personal skills and abilities do you use at work?

3 Describe the type of clothes you wear.

4 Are you working for yourself, as part of a team, for a large or small company? Describe your role.

5 What are you working conditions like? Is your job high powered or do you work in a relaxed atmosphere?

6 If you work with others, describe what they are like. What sort of relationships are you having?

This is no time to question the possibility of there being a perfect job for you. Answer these questions in the best and most imaginative way you can. There is absolutely no point in limiting your beliefs and visualizations; this is what you have been doing all along and this is why you are now unhappy at work. You magnetize whatever you most think about, so take this opportunity to send out strong and specific and vibrant images of you doing your perfect job; magnetize your new reality. As you continue to focus upon your new working conditions you will start to attract changes. Don't be surprised if the new possibilities are not exactly what you had planned; trust the process and give it time and you will be amazed at what can happen!

Setting New Goals

You might have found your vocation but be working for the wrong company; you may be struggling in a job you hate and just want out; you might love the job and the people you work with but you just aren't earning enough money; the job might be tedious but your team may be fantastic; you might have a powerful role and can't stand the pace any more; you might be a frustrated natural leader working in a manual job on a factory production line. There are so many different possibilities that you could be facing, so let's get more specific with some short and long term goals. A few possible examples follow. Write your own goals in your journal.

Short term

To have a more positive attitude towards my job.

To work towards being promoted.

To take some career advice and think about a job change.

To ask for an increase in salary.

To believe that I can earn enough money doing what I find rewarding.

To recognize my true value.

To spend more time doing the things I love to do.

Long term

To improve my relationships with my work colleagues.

To leave my stressful job for something less demanding.

To turn my hobby into a job.

To find a way to balance my mission and my mortgage.

To keep doing the job I love but to find a new company to work for.

To gain the qualifications I need to do the work I would love to do.

Realizing Your Goals

To achieve your goals you must believe in yourself. When we have the personal strength to say 'Yes, I am ready to change', our new beliefs and visualizations can be activated. You can achieve anything that you believe is possible and you have all the energy you need to create a new reality. Replace any doubts and fears with the power of positivity and creativity; the universe supports your every move. The following list of inspirational affirmations will help you to focus on your work goals and to turn them into realities.

Inspirational affirmations

I have a unique contribution to make.

I feel confident at work.

I am a good team player.

I am here to do my life's work.

It is easy to bring my dreams into reality.

I deserve a fabulous job.

I trust the universe to guide and support me.

My boss appreciates me.

I can earn money doing what I love to do.

I love work.

My talents and skills are valuable.

I love my life.

I am a great ... (writer, artist, teacher, actor, whatever).

Changing your work situation might take time and patience. Keep inspiring yourself with these affirmations, they really will keep your spirits up. When I wrote my first book it took a long time and I often found myself wondering things like: Was I a good enough writer? Would I ever finish the book? Would anyone publish it? All marvellous timewasting pursuits, of course, but absolutely death to the creative flow. Whenever self-doubt reared its horns I would type *I am a successful writer* over and over again until I was ready to go on. I used many inspirational affirmations to help me finish that book and without them I really wonder if it would have been completed.

Become inspired to discover your life's work and to realize your full potential, because this is what you were born to do!

Achieving your work goals

When you look at your own personal work goals do you feel highly charged and motivated or do you feel intimidated and low in confidence? If you are feeling scared to change and worried about your abilities, this is absolutely natural. Change implies risk and risk requires trust and sometimes we just feel too wobbly and unsure to trust ourselves. The bigger the change you want to make, the bigger the risk you face; that is the deal. Eleanor Roosevelt had something to say about this that I'm sure will resonate with you. She said, *You must do the thing you think you cannot do.* Remove your own glass ceilings, there are no limitations except those that you believe in. Have you any thought, feeling and behaviour patterns that are stopping you from doing the thing you think you cannot do?

Your mental energy

I'm sure that you will have already uncovered some of your negative thought patterns which might be holding you back. Scarcity consciousness is a great limiter of ability and so is that old non-deserving belief. Did you face any self-doubt when you listed your strengths and skills? Sometimes it's hard to recognize and appreciate our own abilities. There is a very helpful technique that you can use to throw all of your self-doubt into perspective. I want you to imagine that you are your own best friend. Look at yourself objectively; now consider your prospects. You see, you do deserve that terrific job, you do have enormous potential, you are a special and unique person and you have come to do your life's work. Discover it and do it!

Your spiritual energy

Go back to the answers you gave when you were imagining your perfect job. Now, take a few minutes and get into a relaxed state and visualize your answers: what you are wearing to work; how you are getting there; the building you work in and its vibrations. Watch yourself enjoying your working day and feeling so confident and relaxed. Bring that fantastic perfect job into full Technicolor with a soundtrack. Make it all as real as possible.

Recreate this visualization again and again, have no doubt that it is helping you to work magic!

Your emotional energy

Leave behind all those feelings which help to prop up your glass ceilings. Decide to move your energy even if you don't feel like it. When you expand your boundaries and move out of your present comfort zone you may well feel uncomfortable for a while but this will pass. Appreciate yourself for doing things that you think you can't do. Transcend any emotions which stop you moving forward. Feel free to change.

Your physical energy

As you magnetize new work opportunities by the power of your positive beliefs and visualizations, you will find yourself becoming motivated to act in new ways. It often helps to structure your ideas so that you can find the most practical ways to achieve your goals. The following practical plan gives you some guidelines.

Intention: State one of your objectives (I want to . . . .).

Method: Decide what steps you need to take. Put them in the order that they need to be dealt with. You might need some time to think this through.

Needs: List all the resources you might need (help, advice, premises, family support, finances . . . .).

Review: Create some realistic deadlines. Decide on specific dates to check your progress.

Changes: Build some flexibility into your programme so that you can respond creatively to any unforeseen circumstances. Be prepared to change your plans if needs be.

This is a handy structure to use when you need a practical format. Use it for any of your objectives as you move towards realizing your work goals. Remember to take one step at a time and to congratulate yourself for every advance. Positive thoughts and actions can move mountains!

For Discovering Your Life's Work

- Value your skills and strengths.
- Discover what you love to do.
- Allow yourself to be inspired.
- Follow your heart.
- Balance your mission and your mortgage.
- Take charge of the way you earn your living.
- Be prepared to do the thing you think you cannot do.
- Feel free to change.

Conclusion

You are the one and only you: special, unique, amazing and infinitely creative. Always remember that you have the power to change your life and to create new and exciting realities. Honour your dreams and follow your heart and you will then step into your own shoes. You *are* the person you most want to become.

Walk on a rainbow trail;

walk on a trail of song,

and all about you will be beauty.

There is a way out of every dark mist,

over a rainbow trail.

NAVAJO SONG

References and Further Reading

Bek, Lilla and Pullar, Philippa *The Seven Levels of Healing,* Rider, 1986

Ban Breathnach, Sarah, *Simple Abundance,* Bantam Press, 1997

Bryan, Mark, Cameron, Julia and Allen, Catherine, *The Artist's Way at Work,* Pan Books, 1998

Cameron, Julia, *The Vein of Gold,* Pan Books, 1997

Carrington, Hereward, *Your Psychic Powers and How to Develop Them*, The Aquarian Press, 1981

Field, Lynda, *Creating Self-Esteem,* Vermilion, 2001

The Self-Esteem Workbook, Vermilion, 2001

Self-Esteem for Women, Vermilion, 2001

Gawain, Shakti. *Creative Visualization*, Bantam Books, 1985

Living in the Light, Eden Grove Editions, 1988

Gibran, Kahlil, *The Prophet,* Heinemann, 1970

Hay, Louise, *You Can Heal Your Life,* Eden Grove Editions, 1988

Heaner, Martica, *Curves,* Hodder & Stoughton, 1995

Heaven, Ross, *The Journey to You,* Bantam Books, 2001

Koran, Al, *Bring out the Magic in Your Mind,* A. Thomas & Co., 1972

Lang, Doe, *The Charisma Book*, Wyden Books, 1980

McKenna, Paul, *The Hypnotic World of Paul McKenna*, Faber and Faber, 1993

Millman, Dan, *The Warrior Athlete*, Stillpoint Publishing, 1979

Peale, Norman Vincent, *You Can if You Think You Can*, Cedar Books, 1974

Pegg, Mike, *The Positive Workbook*, Enhance, 1995

Redfield, James and Adrienne, Carol, *The Celestine Prophecy: An Experiential Guide*, Bantam Books, 1995

Roman, Sanaya, *Personal Power Through Awareness*, H.J. Kramer, Inc., 1986

Spiritual Growth, H.J. Kramer, Inc., 1989

Roman, Sanaya and Packer, Duane, *Creating Money*, H.J. Kramer, Inc., 1988

Walsch, Neale Donald, *Conversations with God, Book 1*, Hodder & Stoughton, 1995

Conversations With God, Book 3, Hodder & Stoughton, 1998

Wright, Celia, *Higher Nature Health News*, Issue 6

Index

abundance 40-42, 54, 194-196, 201, 203, 206, 207

affirmations 57, 66-68, 76, 90, 95, 128, 153-154, 156, 173, 187-188, 203-204, 205, 219-220

anger 108, 114, 122, 130, 167-168

denial of 108, 168, 170

assertiveness 110-116, 156-157

belief 28-45, 69, 80, 81, 95, 103, 155, 173, 177, 201, 205, 208, 217, 218, 222

core belief 103, 150

blame 14

body language 7

boundaries 162-163, 205-206, 222

brain

alpha waves 63, 66

beta waves 63

left brain 60-61, 69

right brain 60-61, 69

Carrey, Jim 193

challenge 85-87, 94, 159, 189

change 3, 11, 14-17, 21, 35, 37, 42, 43, 58, 66, 72, 88, 89-91, 132-136, 153, 169, 208, 209, 212, 219, 225

fear of 92, 110

childhood 33, 59, 89, 92, 108, 129, 134, 142, 168, 181-182, 211

creating reality 3, 6, 72-83, 109, 121, 132, 147, 215, 217, 225

creativity 132, 156, 194, 214, 219

collective consciousness 51, 53

congruence 144-145

conscious mind 29, 32, 49, 50, 65, 70, 73

cycles 36-39

Cycles of Self-Belief 38

discontent 72

dreams 49

electromagnetism 16-27, 51

Emerson, Ralph Waldo 33

emotion 20, 36, 83, 106-109, 115, 143, 167, 178

fear of 107-108, 167

emotional illiteracy 115

emotional literacy 115

energy 8-13, 15-17, 46, 51, 52, 57, 59, 67, 81, 83, 96, 112, 119, 138, 142, 159, 194, 208

emotional energy 155-156, 174, 188, 191, 206, 222

mental energy 153-154, 173, 187, 189, 204-205, 221

physical energy 156-157, 174, 176-192, 206, 222

spiritual energy 154, 173, 188, 190, 205, 221

exercise 179-180, 183, 185, 189

excuses 183, 189, 190

faith 136-138, 140

families, *see* relationships

fear 107, 115, 119, 120, 125, 134, 140, 195

feelings 20, 36, 80, 81, 106-109, 120, 155-156, 222

fear of 107-108

forgiveness 122-124, 125, 160, 172

Four Principles of Creativity 15-27, 59, 152, 159, 193, 196

freedom 124

friends, *see* relationships

Gandhi 51

Gawain, Shakti, 48

'genie of the lamp' 32, 67, 70, 88

Gibran, Kahlil 208

goals 65-70, 137-138, 140, 151-154, 155, 169-172, 184-190, 202-204, 218-222

guidance 125, 126

guilt 123, 160

harmony 96-114, 145, 187

Hay, Louise 104

healing 177

health and fitness 78, 176-192

Higher Self 146-147

honesty 82

hope 7, 12, 42, 125

hypnotism 28-29, 31

illness 177, 182

imagination 20-21, 36, 57, 59, 62, 68, 69, 155

intimacy 163, 165

intuition 17, 117-119, 125, 128

joy 139

Jung, Carl 17

Koran, Al 39, 199

Life Zone Assessment 77, 148-151, 165, 181, 199, 215

Life Zone Checklist 1-2, 4, 14, 34, 65, 76, 77, 80, 88, 120, 132

Lifeline 119-120

lifestyle 76

love 3, 77, 115-130, 139, 140, 165, 195

magic 14-27, 31, 59, 138, 159, 221

magnetization 15-27, 81, 159-161, 196-197, 207, 215, 222

marriage 129-130, 134-135

materialism 14, 100-101

McKenna, Paul 29

Mind, Body, Spirit and Emotions 4, 85, 97-100, 112, 113, 142, 152, 186

money 3, 79, 193-207

monkeys 48-49

nature 11, 40, 46-48

negativity 2-3, 10, 12, 22, 28, 35-39, 70, 76, 80, 81, 83, 88, 93, 110, 120, 123, 129, 140, 156, 173, 187, 217, 221

nutrition 178-180, 185

obstacles 84-95, 214

opportunity 85-87, 94, 140, 159, 218

parents 33, 75, 134, 168, 200

patterns of behaviour 81, 83, 87-88, 89, 92, 94, 132, 143, 145, 156, 171, 177, 181-183, 200

physical action 109-110

plants 47

positivity 2-3, 6, 7-8, 10, 12, 20, 22, 28, 35-39, 76, 80, 81, 90, 93, 120, 140, 156, 173, 187, 219, 222

relationships 72-73, 85, 91, 158-175, 178

family 3, 33, 75, 76, 142, 158-175

friendships 3, 75, 76, 140, 158-175

love 3, 76, 85, 158-175

work 3, 79, 219

relaxation 63, 68, 124, 174, 180

responsibility 110, 156, 170, 178

risk-taking 136, 137,141

Roosevelt, Eleanor 221

satisfaction levels 1-2

scarcity consciousness 40-42, 43, 54, 195, 201, 203, 207, 221

security 194-195

self-criticism 12

self-doubt 6, 89

self-image 34, 77, 103, 113, 142-157, 143-144

self-knowledge 88, 89

slugs 46, 48

spirituality 100-101, 113, 115-117, 124-130, 146-147

'stickiness' 22, 42

subpersonalities 143-144, 146

suffering 10

synchronicity 16, 17, 25-26, 117, 136

telepathy 52-56

Thoreau, Henry David 84

thought 18-20, 33-35, 39-45, 52-56, 66, 83, 143

unconscious mind 29, 31, 32, 49, 50, 65, 70

victims 42, 75-76, 82, 85, 91, 93, 107, 109, 110, 119, 124, 135, 147, 155, 156, 161-162

visualization 57-70, 76, 90, 124-125, 138, 156, 174, 188, 205-206, 218, 222

wealth 193-207

work 79, 178, 208-223

world view 41-42